# THE
# SECRET OF
# SUPERNATURAL
# LIVING

# THE
# SECRET OF
# SUPERNATURAL
# LIVING

BY

## Adrian Rogers

THOMAS NELSON PUBLISHERS
NASHVILLE • CAMDEN • NEW YORK

Third printing

Scripture quotations are from the King James Version of the Bible.

Published in Nashville, Tennessee, by Thomas Nelson, Inc., Publishers
and distributed in Canada by Lawson Falle, Ltd., Cambridge, Ontario.

Printed in the United States of America.

Library of Congress Cataloging in Publication Data

Rogers, Adrian.
    The secret of supernatural living.

        1. Christian life—1960-          I. Title.
BV4501.2.R63   1982      248.4      82-8060
ISBN 0-8407-5270-9                   AACR2

# Contents

# Preface

Where on earth does God live? It has taken me quite a while to discover the answer to that question. But the discovery has changed my life.

In these pages I want to share with you some truths that are helping me to maturity in Christ. They all revolve around the central truth that I am now a temple of God and He lives in me.

I don't want to be simplistic. But I do, by the grace of God, want to be clear.

Sometimes when we hear a man of letters speak with double-jointed words and obscure terms, we say, "Oh, he must be brilliant. I didn't understand him." Not necessarily so! A muddy river is not always deep. The common people heard Jesus gladly. For the learned, those wise in the philosophies of men, the message was often missed.

The Lord Jesus found me when I was a teen-age boy. I had never been in serious trouble as a boy, but I am sure I gave my parents a fair share of heartaches. My folks were good, hard-working, salt-of-the-earth kind of people. Dad earned his living in the automobile and furniture business. I had my share of whippings. Dad always said it was because he loved me. I have often thought that if that is so, I must have been his favorite child. I got far more of this love than the rest of the kids!

But, like all of us, I needed something more in life than parental example and discipline. At an old-fashioned revival crusade in West Palm Beach, Florida, our hometown, my dad stepped out to give his heart and life to Christ. I followed right behind him. I believe that an eternal change took place in those moments, and that night I became a new creature in Christ. But I was not well-instructed on how to live the Christian life.

Old habits and ways die hard. The cheating in class, the school-yard fights, truancy, bad language, and disobedience still pulled at me. I was up and down in my Christian life for over a year, and I was miserable. A Christian out of step with his Lord can be more miserable than an unbeliever, I found out.

One night after I had walked my girl friend home from church, I stopped and prayed. I was tired of the struggle, the doubt, the failure. Also, I had by this time learned more of the truth of God. I had learned that salvation was entirely by God's grace and could only be received by faith. God was showing me that salvation was not a reward for righteous people, but a gift for the guilty ones. "Lord Jesus," I said, looking straight up into the starry heavens, "I don't know if I am a true Christian and the devil is trying to make me doubt it or if I am still lost and the Holy Spirit is bringing me under conviction, but the one thing I do know is that I am miserable. I need to get some things settled with You for all eternity. I want to know that I am in Your kingdom and right with You."

Then I said, "Lord Jesus, right now with all of my heart, once and for all, now and forever, I trust You and You alone to save me according to the promise of Your Word. If I have never really trusted You, I do so now. If I am already saved, then I reaffirm it. But one thing I know is that I am driving down a spiritual peg tonight. I do not ask for feeling. I stand upon Your promise, Lord Jesus, and I know that settles it!"

At that moment, a wonderful river of God's peace and assurance began to flow through my heart and, praise His name, it has never stopped flowing.

As a young man, I had thought seriously about being a lawyer or an architect. But now I knew that God had a right to make these choices in my life. He would lead me into His will and He would decide for the best. "Lord, whatever You want me to do, I'll do it. Just let me know," I prayed.

I'm not sure exactly how the "germ-thought" that God might want me to preach got into my heart. But I found it there. "Lord, do You really want me to preach?" I would ask Him. As a high-school football player, I was not afraid of much that moved on the gridiron, but the thought of being a public speaker was disturbing. More candidly, it scared me to death.

Yet, this little seed of a thought would not go away. For weeks I would pray like this: "Lord, I think You want me to preach." Then for days I would pray, "Lord, if You don't want me to preach, You had better let me know." Finally it was, "Lord, You are calling me, and I know it."

I made a public commitment, and it was settled. From that point on I did not look back. I was thrilled—and still am—that God would call me to serve Him. My high school sweetheart, who is now my wife, was also thrilled. In her heart, she sensed God calling her into His full-time service as well.

As a would-be preacher, I knew I needed God's might and power in my life. I also knew I was totally inadequate. I had not heard much about the power of God available to the Christian, but I knew I needed something.

Our home was near the field where we practiced football. I went alone to that field one night to seek the Lord. It was a beautiful South Florida summer night. I walked and prayed,

"Lord Jesus, I want You to use me." Then I knelt down and repeated, "Lord Jesus, I want You to use me." Then, wanting to humble myself before Him, I stretched out prostrate, face down on the grass and said, "Lord Jesus, I am Yours. Please use me." That still did not seem low enough. So I made a hole in the dirt and placed my nose into it. "Lord Jesus, I am as low as I know how to get. Please use me."

(I did not know it then, but I learned later the English word "humble" comes from a Latin root *humus* meaning "ground" or "earth.")

Again, something happened in my life that night. I didn't have ecstasies or a vision of any kind, but there was a transformation. At that time, I knew very little theology. But I would be less than honest to deny that God graciously released His power into my young heart and life. There was a great joy present and a desire to share Christ with everyone.

Shortly after that time, I entered college and was asked to serve as pastor of a small country church. I was nineteen years of age and utterly untrained. I am sure my preaching was greatly lacking in form and content, but God graciously and visibly worked. I was often surprised at His power. There were commitments for repentance and tears of joy from the start in that little congregation. People were brought to Christ in unusual numbers for such a small church and town. There was no mistaking the mighty hand of God.

Then I married Joyce, my high-school sweetheart. And we served together in that little church until I finished my college work. After three years we tearfully resigned that precious country church to go on to seminary.

By this time I had gained some small repute as a "boy-preacher" and had learned a little theology. I must confess, however, that I began to coast spiritually. I gradually began to shift my dependence upon the Lord—*along with* my trust in the Lord—to clever methods and human ability. I did not know it then, but as I look back now, I realize I had lost that glow and power I had at first known. I knew more in my head, but the same power from God was not there in my heart.

After seminary Joyce and I were called back to Florida to a fine little church in Fort Pierce. By this time we had had three children: Stephen, Gayle, and Phillip. Phillip was only two months old when we got settled in the new parsonage.

It happened on Mother's Day. It was a beautiful day as the days in May so often are near the Florida coast. I had just preached a Mother's Day message on the blessings of a Christian home. Our small house was nestled right next door to the little white cement-block church. Joyce was out in the kitchen preparing our lunch after the service. I was in the living room reading.

Suddenly, I heard her distraught voice. "Adrian," she cried, "Come here quickly! Something is wrong with Phillip!"

I leaped to my feet. She had our baby boy in her arms. He was not breathing. His face had a blue cast upon it.

"What's wrong?" she cried.

"I don't know. You call the hospital and tell them I am coming."

I took our little boy and put him inside my coat to keep him warm. With eyes blinded by tears, I screeched out of our driveway and sped on to the hospital emergency room. "Please help me," I cried to an awaiting nurse as I burst through the heavy double-entrance doors to the hospital. Kind hands took Phillip and rushed him into a nearby room. I kneeled outside that emergency-room door and prayed for God's mercy, not caring who saw me or what they might think.

After a while, an attending doctor came out of the room, without Phillip, and walked over to me. "He's gone," he said as he laid his hand on my shoulder and shook his head. "There was nothing we could do. We tried."

It was one of those sudden "crib deaths."

Joyce was standing in the doorway of our house when I returned alone. The look on my face told the story. Mother's Day had turned into incredible grief and confusion for us. We had not known death in either of our families. It was so sudden. And so stark. We did the only thing we knew to do. We kneeled and called out to the Lord for help.

Then we turned to the Word of God. I wasn't sure just where to begin reading. Instead, the Lord Himself led us to the message we so sorely needed. This is what God said:

> Grace be to you and peace from God our Father, and from the Lord Jesus Christ. Blessed be God, even the Father of our Lord Jesus Christ, the Father of mercies, and the God of all comfort; Who comforteth us in all our tribulation, that we may be able to comfort them which are in any trouble, by the comfort wherewith we ourselves are comforted of God (2 Cor. 1:2–4).

I did not understand all that God was allowing to happen to us. But He had already made one thing abundantly clear. The Father of mercies was going to use the sorrow in our lives to make a blessing to other people with broken hearts. We gave our brokenness and confusion to the God of all comfort.

That Sunday afternoon we drove to our parents' homes. The church had gotten someone to fill the pulpit for me for the evening service. The services were just beginning as we backed out of the driveway. I can still hear the congregation today as they were singing, "No never alone, no never alone, He promised never to leave me, never to leave me alone."

Joyce and I *willed* to worship the Lord together, and we sang every praise song we knew as we drove those sixty miles back to our hometown. And it was so very true. We were not alone! God's presence was never more real.

In the days and months that followed, we sought the Lord in a new way. Then, by God's grace, a friend and fellow-pastor came to our church and preached a message on the Spirit-filled life. Our hungry hearts reached up and received the truth, and again the transformation took place. The Lord Jesus came with a new fullness and freshness. I discovered that Jesus Christ truly was alive in me and was just waiting to take over.

I realize now that the experience of God's fullness in me that I received then was *the same power I had already received* as a young preacher who prayed that night on the football practice field. I had just come back to where I used to be. The difference now, however, was that I understood more of the theology behind it all.

I would not for anything minimize theology. But I learned that one can sometimes experience Christ without a full understanding of Christian theology. And sadly enough, one can know theology and not experience the power of God. Best, of course, is to experience Christ's life as confirmed by and conformed to the Word of God. Basically, this is what I want to gain for you as I write this book.

One of God's great ways of communicating spiritual truth so it is easily understood is by use of illustrations. The Bible abounds with these. Jesus used illustrations over and over again as He taught. The vine and the branches, a farmer's field, a pearl are but a few examples.

One of the clearest illustrations and object lessons of spiritual truth is the Old Testament temple. This magnificent building, constructed according to a precise pattern, was given by the Master Teacher to help us grasp spiritual truth. Therefore, as we consider our experience of Christ, we will do so in light of what I call "temple truth."

Don't wrinkle your brow. This is not going to be a heady or complicated study of the intricate details of the temple. Nor will it be dry-as-dust historical study of the Bible. Our study, as you will note, is really about *you,* and the victory that God has provided for you.

The marvelous truth is that *we* are temples of the Holy Spirit as clearly stated by the apostle Paul, "What? know ye not that your body is the temple of the Holy Ghost which is in you, which ye have of God, and ye are not your own?" (1 Cor. 6:19).

In the Old Testament, God had a temple for His people. In the New Testament, He has a people for His temple. Our very bodies are a holy temple. The Lord Himself is the royal Resident who lives within us.

This truth of the fullness of the indwelling God is so very vital and valuable to you. Understand it and it will change your life from the monotonous to the momentous. There is no greater truth than to discover that the great God of glory has condescended to indwell mortals such as we. "Christ in you, the hope of glory." (Col. 1:27).

Let these words, true as they are, become a bright, living reality in you, and you will discover the key that unlocks the treasure house of a thousand other spiritual riches. Drabness and discouragement will be a thing of the past. To be sure, there will still be problems. But Christian reality and victory over these problems will be the note of the day.

# A Royal
# Residence

*And the very God of peace sanctify you wholly; and I pray God
your whole spirit and soul and body be preserved blameless unto
the coming of our Lord Jesus Christ (1 Thess. 5:23).*

I have observed that most people are not all that concerned about going to heaven or hell (they should be, but
they are not). What they want is meaning to life. They are
concerned with "how to hack it on Monday." They are
looking for life—full and abundant, here and now. That life
is available in Christ.

Devotional writers have come up with many terms to
describe it. It has been called the Life of Victory, the Deeper
Life, The Wider Life, Life on the Highest Plane, and other
things. These all say something about the life our Lord
offers, but when it is all said and done, perhaps the best
term, when rightly understood, is just—*the Christian life!*

## Man—A House of Three Rooms

When God designed the Old Testament temple, He designed it with three major parts or sections. There was the
*outer court*, which could be seen by all and visited by all. It
was here in the outer court that external worship took place.

Next, and further in, was the *holy place*. It was a more

restricted place where only the priests could go for worship and service to God.

Last, there was the *holy of holies*. It was the innermost court. It was absolutely off limits except for the high priest, who was a prefiguring of Jesus. He would enter once a year to make atonement for the people. In this intimate and secret inner sanctum, God dwelt in His shekinah glory.

This house of three rooms conformed to a precise pattern. This is seen in the tabernacle, which was a prototype for the temple. "According to all that I show thee, after the pattern of the tabernacle, and the pattern of all the instruments thereof, even so shall ye make it" (Ex. 25:9).

Also note the directions given by David to Solomon for the construction of the temple.

> Then David gave to Solomon his son the pattern of the porch, and of the houses thereof, and of the treasuries thereof, and of the upper chambers thereof, and of the inner parlors thereof, and of the place of the mercy seat, And the pattern of all that he had by the spirit, of the courts of the house of the Lord, and of all the chambers round about, of the treasuries of the house of God, and of the treasuries of the dedicated things (1 Chr. 28:11,12).

The reason for all of this precision is that the tabernacle and temple were to be grand object-lessons. They were to teach us something of the nature of God and the nature of man.

One reason for this grouping into three areas is that the God we know and worship is a triune Being, one God in three distinct Persons—Father, Son, and Holy Spirit.

In fact, as we look at the world around us, we can see all that God has created reflects the Holy Trinity in some way. For example, all space is triune in dimension: height, width, and depth. Each dimension is distinct from the other two, and yet all three are a part of the same, and no part exists without the other.

The same thing is true about time. Time is triune. It consists of past, present, and future. One element of time never exists without the other two but is always distinct from them. Together they make up one basic entity—time.

There is some truth that we can know only by revelation. This is not because it is contrary to reason, but it may indeed be beyond reason. We sometimes must lay our intellectual pride in the dust and accept a Bible truth by faith.

Men have raced their theological motors to try to find an adequate, rational illustration of the Holy Trinity. There are many such illustrations, but they all break down somewhere. And, personally, I am glad they do. Why? The one true God—Father, Son, and Holy Spirit—is absolutely unique. Therefore, God cannot be truly compared to, or illustrated by, anything.

"To whom then will ye liken me, or shall I be equal? saith the Holy One" (Is. 40:25).

This is why early Christians often used the word *mystery* as they referred to the Holy Trinity. We couldn't have any confidence in a God who could be fully explained or comprehended by our finite minds, but we can have great joy in a God who can be experienced and known.

Man, as the highest expression of God's creation, also reflects his Creator's triune nature. "And the very God of peace sanctify you wholly; and I pray God your whole *spirit* and *soul* and *body* be preserved blameless unto the coming of our Lord Jesus Christ" (1 Thess. 5:23, italics mine). The threefold nature of man is seen in that he is spirit, soul, and body.

Interestingly, the Old Testament temple illustrates the New Testament truth of the triune nature of man. The

Christian is God's temple, God's dwelling place. "What, know ye not that your body is the temple of the Holy Ghost which is in you, which ye have of God, and ye are not your own" (1 Cor. 6:19). It could be said that we are a house of three rooms.

Now before I proceed further, let me say a word to any theologians who may be reading these words. I am aware that some theologians prefer to think of man as a dichotomy, or as having only two parts to his nature—the body as the tangible part and the soul and the spirit lumped together as the intangible part. There is some truth to this approach, but on the other hand, the Bible still speaks clearly of spirit, soul, and body. The spirit and soul may never be separated, and they do not operate independently of the other, but they certainly may be differentiated.

You were created to know three worlds—the spiritual world, the psychological world, and the material world. Roughly speaking, we can think of these as the world above us, the world within us, and the world beneath us.

These three worlds are related to the three parts of our human nature—spirit, soul, and body. Understand this and many wonderful truths will come into focus. When a man is rightly related to the material world with his body, he is *healthy*. When he is rightly related to the psychological world with his soul, he is *happy*. When he is properly related to the spiritual world with his spirit, he is *holy*. God's aim is that ultimately we are to experience all three realities: health, happiness, and holiness.

## The Outer Man and the Material World

The body is what the Bible calls the "outward man." "For which cause we faint not; but though our outward man perish, yet the inward man is renewed day by day" (2 Cor.

4:16). The human body corresponds to the outer part of the temple. That outer court of the temple was the place of sacrifice, and our bodies are the place of sacrifice. Paul tells that they are to be presented as a "living sacrifice." (Rom. 12:1).

It is not, by the way, true Christian thought to view the body as sinful or evil. The body is God's creation and should be presented to Him as a holy temple. Most of us need to realize this and thereby do a better job of temple maintenance.

Yet, on the other hand, we do not need to overestimate the importance of the body. It is not your body, as we will see shortly, that gives you supreme value. Animals also have bodies—and so do vegetables. Man is much more than a toad or a turnip.

## The Inner Man and the Psychological World

The soul is a bit more difficult for us to understand, if for no other reason than that it is invisible. The soul is that psychological part of our nature or human personality that lives in our body or "earthly house."

The Greek word for soul is *psuche*. It is the same word from which we get "psychic," "psychology," and other related words. Generally speaking, therefore, we could say the soul is the psychological part of man and consists primarily of *mind, emotion*, and *will*. The Bible illustrates and catalogs the activity and function of the soul quite carefully.

The soul, we read, is centered in *the mind*. "So shall the knowledge of wisdom be unto thy soul: when thou hast found it, then there shall be a reward, and thy expectation shall not be cut off" (Prov. 24:14).

The soul is the center of the *emotions*. "And it came to pass, when he had made an end of speaking unto Saul, that the soul of Jonathan was knit with the soul of David, and Jonathan loved him as his own soul" (1 Sam. 18:1).

And the soul is the center of the *will.* "The things that my soul refused to touch are as my sorrowful meat" (Job 6:7).

We must not think of the soul as being inherently evil or unredeemable. Mind, emotion, and will are only evil as they have been corrupted through sin. The soul itself was created by God that through it we might understand Him, love Him, and serve Him. Thus, when we turn to the Lord, we are never called to crush or surpress our minds or wills or even our emotions. Instead, our souls (as do our bodies and human spirits) come into union with Christ. As David says of the Lord, "He restoreth my soul . . ." (Ps. 23:3).

The soul is the real you living inside your earthly house. When you look at me, all you really see with your eyes is the house (the body) that I live in. Woodrow Wilson's favorite limerick went like this:

> *I know how ugly I are,*
> *I know my face ain't no star,*
> *But I don't mind it,*
> *'Cause I'm behind it;*
> *It's the fellow in front*
> *Who gets the jar.*

## The Innermost Man and the Spiritual World

The human spirit, in the biblical sense of the word, is a mystery. What I mean by that is it could never be discovered by human ingenuity. We know that man has a spirit, through the revelation of God's two-edged Sword. There is no surgical scalpel sharp enough to separate the spirit from the soul except the living Word of God.

"For the word of God is quick, and powerful, and sharper than any two-edged sword, piercing even to the dividing asunder of soul and spirit, and of the joints and marrow, and is a discerner of the thoughts and intents of the heart" (Heb. 4:12).

The uniqueness of man is seen in that he has a spirit. Animals, by contrast, can be spoken of as having bodies and souls, but they are void of spirit. God describes the creation of the animals this way: "And God said, Let the earth bring forth the living creature after his kind, cattle, and creeping thing, and beast of the earth after his kind: and it was so" (Gen. 1:24). The Hebrew word translated "creature" in this verse is *nephesh* and is usually translated "soul." It means self-conscious life, as opposed to plant life, which is without soul or spirit.

Plants and animals have bodies. Animals also have souls. So what makes a man unique? It is his spirit. When God made man, He breathed into him the "breath of life" (Gen. 2:7). This breath of life became the human spirit. The words "breath" and "spirit" are used interchangeably in the Bible. Man was endowed with a spiritual nature and thus the glorious ability to know and worship God. God did not breathe this special breath of life into any other of His creatures.

Note again, this is why the apostle writes as he does: "And the very God of peace sanctify you wholly; and I pray God your whole spirit and soul and body be preserved blameless unto the coming of our Lord Jesus Christ" (1 Thess. 5:23).

### How to Function With Unction

Now, what is the function of the human spirit? It is the part of man's nature that enables him to know God and to worship Him. Mary said, "And my spirit hath rejoiced in God my Saviour" (Luke 1:47). Jesus told the woman at the well, "But the hour cometh, and now is, when the true worshipers shall worship the Father in spirit and in truth: for the Father seeketh such to worship him" (John 4:23). The apostle Paul wrote, "The Spirit itself beareth witness with our spirit, that we are the children of God" (Rom. 8:16).

Animals will never pray, never seek God, never worship because they have no spirit. That which keeps man from being more than a clever animal, with the ability to talk and walk upright, is his spirit. That which brings dignity to the soul of man—making it worth more than the whole wide world—is that it is inseparably linked to his spirit. The soul of an animal may perish, but man's soul, forever linked with his spirit, will go on—endless, timeless, dateless. Man's soul is worth more than all of the world because man, through his spirit, can know and worship and enjoy God.

The Bible has described the human spirit as a lamp. "The spirit of man is the candle of the Lord, searching all the inward parts of the belly" (Prov. 20:27). The function of the human spirit is to give light to the temple of man's body. The word translated "candle" is better translated "lamp." A candle burns its own substance, but a lamp must be fed with oil. The oil that feeds the lamp of the human spirit is the Holy Spirit. Thus, we are given illumination through the power of the Holy Spirit working in the human spirit.

So here is how God created a man in order that he might *function with unction*. The Father's intention is that you and I be joined to Christ in order that the Holy Spirit may illuminate or enlighten our human spirit. Then, our human spirit is to communicate God's divine will to our soul (mind, emotion, and will), and the soul is to motivate the body to navigate out into the world. These three, always working together, serve to make you what we can rightly call a man or woman of God.

When we belong to Christ, man's body will be a visible representation of the will and working of the invisible God, and our invisible God will then receive the glory due to His name. Jesus said, "Let your light so shine before men, that they may see your good works, and glorify your Father which is in heaven" (Matt. 5:16).

Let me ask you a question: Is Jesus Christ in control of your life right now? Are you experiencing the love of God the Father and the communion and presence of the Holy Spirit?

Perhaps you have slid into the same sort of humdrum existence that had sneaked up on me and made me its captive—relying on my own power and abilities, rather than upon the power and gifts of God. If that is true, I beg you to put this book aside for a few moments and turn to the Lord in prayer. Confess to Him that you have wrongly taken charge of your life, and invite the Holy Spirit to fill you and direct you once again. Go back to that childlike simplicity of faith and trust in the Lord that you knew from the start.

Now let us sum up. Man is a house of three rooms. The Old Testament temple is an illustration of that fact. The inner-most room or the holy of holies corresponds to man's spirit, where the very presence of God should dwell with all of His fullness. Does the great God live in your house? He has said, "For thus saith the high and lofty One that inhabiteth eternity, whose name is Holy; I dwell in the high and holy place, with him also that is of a contrite and humble spirit, to revive the spirit of the humble, and to revive the heart of the contrite ones" (Is. 57:15).

Ian Thomas has put it so well:

> To be in Christ—that is redemption; but for Christ to be in you—that is sanctification! To be in Christ—that makes you fit for heaven; but for Christ to be in you—that makes you fit for earth! To be in Christ—that changes your destination; but for Christ to be in you—that changes your destiny! The one makes heaven your home—the other makes this world His workshop.[1]

# Supernaturally Natural

*Let the word of Christ dwell in you richly in all wisdom; teaching and admonishing one another in psalms and hymns and spiritual songs, singing with grace in your hearts to the Lord. And whatsoever ye do in word or deed, do all in the name of the Lord Jesus, giving thanks to God and the Father by him.*

*Wives, submit yourselves unto your own husbands, as it is fit in the Lord. Husbands, love your wives, and be not bitter against them. Children, obey your parents in all things: for this is well-pleasing unto the Lord. Fathers, provoke not your children to anger, lest they be discouraged.*

*Servants, obey in all things your masters according to the flesh; not with eyeservice, as men-pleasers, but in singleness of heart, fearing God. And whatsoever ye do, do it heartily, as to the Lord, and not unto men; Knowing that of the Lord ye shall receive the reward of the inheritance: for ye serve the Lord Christ. But he that doeth wrong shall receive for the wrong which he hath done, and there is no respect of persons (Col. 3:16–25).*

One of the curses of twentieth-century Christianity is Sunday-morning religion.

> *They're praising God on Sunday,*
> *They'll be all right on Monday,*
> *It's just a little habit they've acquired.*

But as temples of the Holy Spirit, we are not to be victims of Sunday religion. We are to be living sixty minutes an hour, twenty-four hours a day, and three hundred and sixty-five days a year in the Spirit, worshiping and serving the Lord.

The common idea of worship is that we leave the secular world outside and go into a church house to worship. And then, because we are in church, we suddenly begin to behave like someone we're not. The sign over the church door where I attended as a boy said, "The Lord is in His holy temple. Let all of the earth keep silence." I mistakenly took that to mean that I had just entered the holy temple and had better start acting religious.

Oh, that someone had taught me that that pile of bricks was not a temple of God, but that we, His people, are. Of course, we are to be reverent in a church service and should respect the place where we are meeting, but that is not the point at all.

I needed to learn that, as a Christian, no longer could I neatly divide my life up in two divisions—the secular and the sacred. Notice the key verse in the above Scripture. "And whatsoever ye do in word or deed, do all in the name of the Lord Jesus, giving thanks to God and the Father by him" (Col. 3:17).

"Whatsoever ye do" means everything, and therefore, everything is to be done in the name of Jesus. That includes all of life. The secular is to be sanctified so that Jesus will be glorified in everything. Because He now lives in me, every day is a holy day, every time is a sacred time, and every task is to be done for the honor and glory of Christ. The spiritual life is seven days a week.

Have you ever gone to a church service where people "acted spiritual"? They get a stained-glass look on their faces and speak in funeral-home tones. Even the minister, who at the church picnic seems normal enough, stands in the pulpit and entones "dearly beloved" as if he just swallowed the communion rail.

Yet, when the service is over and this sanctified throng reaches the cafeteria line over at the shopping center, they seem to be amazingly normal people. They have changed from the spiritual mode to the secular mode like someone had thrown a switch. The entire idea seems artificial, does it not?

Because we are indwelt by the Holy Spirit, that line between the secular and the spiritual in our lives is erased. We don't need to "act" spiritual, because we are spiritual. We are a temple of God on a full-time basis. Therefore, in all natural things we are to be spiritual, and in all spiritual things we are to be natural. A Spirit-filled Christian will be *naturally supernatural, and yet supernaturally natural.* Everything is to be done in the name of Jesus.

What does it mean, therefore, to do everything in the name of Jesus? It means at least three things to me.

## Do Everything With the Approval of Jesus

In the Bible, as well as in life today, a man's name and his character are linked.

One of the techniques that Madison Avenue uses in merchandising is to have a well-known personality endorse a product. He lends his name and reputation to the product. The way this frequently is done is for the celebrity to have his name inscribed upon some piece of merchandise. Many a little boy has wanted a specific baseball bat because his big-league hero had his name stamped upon it. That superstar was saying, in effect, "I approve this baseball bat. It is consistent with the standards that I hold as a professional athlete."

In a similar way, to do everything in the name of Jesus

means to do only that which He could endorse or approve. All that we do should be consistent with His character. We ought to do nothing that we could not sign His name to.

If name means character, then the character of Jesus, and not some set of rules, is the standard for our Christian life. The Bible is not primarily a rule book with a list of dos and don'ts.

Rules are for kids. The more immature a child is, the more rules his parents must lay down for him. "Don't play with matches." "Come straight home from school." "Practice your music every day for forty-five minutes." The more mature child does not need rules like this. He is able to comprehend what his parents desire and, therefore, tries to live so as to honor their characters. The greater the maturity, the fewer the rules.

What a joy it is to me as a father when one of my children faces a situation about which we have not specifically talked and no rules have been laid down, yet he comes through with flying colors. "Daddy, I just did what I thought you would have wanted me to do. I knew you would approve." What he does is what he feels is consistent with my character.

This is such a higher plane of living. One may find loopholes in rules.

A lawyer reported to his client in a divorce case, "Mrs. Blake, I've succeeded in making a settlement with your husband that is eminently fair to both of you."

"Fair to *both!*" exploded Mrs. Blake. "I could have done that myself! What do you think I hired a lawyer for?"

One may twist the law, but he will never find a loophole in the character of Jesus. Therefore, the Bible is not primarily a book of minute laws, but of great principles: chief among them is Do all in the name of Jesus. We ought to be able to sign His name to our every action.

## Do Everything in the Authority of Jesus

Not only does name stand for approval, but it also stands for authority. The name signed on a check gives the banker the authority to pay certain funds out of that account if the check bears the name of a person who has money in the bank.

A policeman who weighs 140 pounds may stand before a semi-truck and, with an uplifted hand, say, "Stop, in the name of the law." He is appealing to an authority higher than himself. The truck stops because of that name or authority. The policeman certainly did not and could not stop the truck with physical force. His badge and his uniform carry the authority of the government he represents.

We need to learn a lesson right here. Our authority over Satan does not rest in the fact that we are stronger than he is. We indeed are not. Yet when Jesus sent out His disciples, He said to them, "Behold, I give unto you power to tread on serpents and scorpions, and over all the power of the enemy: and nothing shall by any means hurt you" (Luke 10:19). While the King James Version gives it this way, it literally says, "Behold, I have given you authority . . . over all the power of the enemy."

Note the difference between power and authority. The policeman stops the truck with authority, not with power. Likewise we overcome Satan not with power, but with authority.

Remembering that name stands for authority, we then understand more fully what it means to pray in the name of Jesus. To pray in His name does not necessarily mean that we close our prayers with a little formula, "In Jesus' name. Amen." I cannot find any prayer in the Bible that ends that way. I'm not saying that it's wrong to close a prayer in that manner, but that is not what Jesus meant when He taught us to pray in His name.

The prayer in Jesus' name is a prayer that has His authority behind it. And remember that name means approval as well as authority. Therefore, I can guarantee you no prayer will have His authority if it does not first of all have His approval. There are too many spiritual forgers signing Jesus' name to their prayer checks, but they will not be honored at the bank of heaven. There is no authority because there is no approval.

Are you living every day with the authority of Christ in your life? Every day and every deed ought to be lived with this conscious authority. You ought to do your housework, rear your children, earn your salary, and enjoy your leisure time with the authority of His mighty name. Every effort ought to be crowned with the power of heaven.

### Under and Over

Let me say here that we can never have this authority from Him to live as we ought until we are first of all submitted to Him. One of the greatest lessons I have ever learned—and I'm still learning—is that I cannot be *over* until I'm willing to be *under*. I cannot have authority until I'm first of all submitted to authority.

In the seventh chapter of the Gospel of Luke is an amazing story. A Roman army officer had a servant that was gravely ill. He wanted Jesus to heal this servant, and Jesus was coming to the house to do just this. The centurion, however, sent a message to Jesus while He was still outside the house.

> Then Jesus went with them. And when he was now not far from the house, the centurion sent friends to him, saying unto

him, Lord, trouble not thyself: for I am not worthy that thou shouldest enter under my roof: Wherefore neither thought I myself worthy to come unto thee: but say in a word, and my servant shall be healed. For I also am a man set under authority, having under me soldiers, and I say unto one, Go, and he goeth; and to another, Come, and he cometh; and to my servant, Do this, and he doeth it.

When Jesus heard these things, he marveled at him, and turned about, and said unto the people that followed him, I say unto you, I have not found so great faith, no, not in Israel. And they that were sent, returning to the house, found the servant whole that had been sick (Luke 7:6–10).

This man had such a rare insight into the principles of spiritual authority that Jesus marveled at him. He was a Gentile, but what an understanding of spiritual authority he had. As an army officer, he understood the principle of authority. He could command those soldiers under him, and they would go and come. This would continue to be true as long as he stayed under those who were over him. But should he step out from under this authority, he would lose the authority that was his to exercise over those under him.

The centurion then applied this principle to the work of Jesus. He said, in effect, "Jesus, because of your submission to the Father over you, you have authority over this sickness. Just speak a word and my servant will be healed."

The principle is clearly taught. We have authority when we are under authority. We forfeit authority when we refuse to submit to the authority that God has set over us. We cannot be over unless we are willing to be under.

Oh, the heartbreaking tragedy of those who are living without the authority of God in their lives. There are pathetic preachers who preach without authority because they will not submit to the authority of the Word of God. They are the "bland" leading the "bland."

There are failing fathers who have no spiritual authority in the home because they have not submitted to the lordship of Christ and to their elders in the church. Multitudes of mothers have no authority over their children because they will not submit to their own husbands as unto the Lord.

Think of the Christian young people who have no victory over the sins of the world, the flesh, and the devil, because they are rebelling against their parents.

Many Christians, who ought to be victorious in their prayer life and have victory over the devil, are in a state of disarray because they are rebelling against the spiritual leadership that God has set up in the church.

It is so clearly taught in the Bible and yet so rarely practiced in the world. We are not exercising our God-given authority because we have not submitted to the authority of Jesus.

We must know the restraint of the Spirit before we can know the release of the Spirit. When we teach our children to drive, we teach them first about the brakes and then about the accelerator. God the Holy Spirit first teaches restraint, and then gives release.

## Do Everything for the Acclaim of Jesus

Name means more than approval and authority. It also means acclaim or honor. On occasion, I have received a note telling me that a gift has been given to a certain cause in my name. That was the donor's way of saying that it was given in my honor or for my acclaim. I have learned to pass such honors on to Jesus. If we can learn to pass the praise on to Jesus, we can pass the criticism on to Him also—the unjust criticism, that is.

You see, as the temple of the Spirit of God, my life must be lived for only one purpose—that He will be glorified. Consider the words of the apostle Peter. "If any man speak, let him speak as the oracles of God; if any man minister, let him do it as of the ability which God giveth: that God in all things may be glorified through Jesus Christ, to whom be praise and dominion forever and ever. Amen" (1 Pet. 4:11). And Paul echoes the same truth. "Whether therefore ye eat, or drink, or whatsoever ye do, do all to the glory of God" (1 Cor. 10:31).

As one who is indwelt by the Holy Spirit, you carry a tremendous responsibility to God and to man. If, indeed, the sign on your house says Under New Management, you are *de facto* on display.

It is only the life that is lived with the approval of Jesus and in the authority of Jesus that will bring acclaim to Jesus. To live in the Spirit and to do everything in the name of Jesus means that we will do nothing to dishonor His name.

Just think what would happen if Christians started living this kind of a life every day and in every place. When God's people realize that they are to be naturally supernatural and supernaturally natural, the world will begin to take notice. The best argument for Christianity and the best argument against Christianity is the life of a Christian. Not only are we to be His witnesses. We ought to be a part of the evidence!

# The Anatomy
# of Salvation

*A little girl was supposed to take her birth certificate to school.
Her mother had solemnly warned her not to lose it because of its
tremendous importance. But lose it she did. Later, she was sitting
on the steps of the schoolhouse crying. The janitor asked her what
was wrong. She replied, "I lost my excuse for being born."*

Anybody who does not enjoy the fullness of salvation in
Christ has indeed lost his excuse for being born again. Since
salvation is our very basis for the Holy Spirit to come and to
live within us, I want to establish in this chapter what is the
fullness of our salvation in Christ and review something of
the glory of what is available to the child of God. In the last
chapter we surveyed the house. Here we will look at the
work of the Builder and Designer.

I like the word "saved." For some reason sophisticated
theologians want to steer away from that word because they
think it sounds too common—language that belongs under
the revival tent. But it is a good word. Furthermore, it is a
biblical word. And the only alternative to being saved is
being lost.

Sometimes a good way to understand what it means to be
saved is to first understand what it means to be lost. To be
lost is to be in a state of spiritual death.

This spiritual death is best illustrated in the experience of

Adam. His death and our deaths are linked. "In Adam all die" (1 Cor. 15:22). Well if we died in Adam, just how did Adam die?

You will recall that God had placed Adam and Eve in the Garden of Eden and given them all that they needed to be healthly, happy, and holy. He had made ample provision for Adam—body, soul, and spirit. At that time God Himself lived as a royal Resident in His first temple named Adam.

But in order for man to have the ability to truly love God, He had to have the opportunity to choose not to love God. A choice had to be given. God describes the basis of that choice.

> And the Lord God took the man, and put him into the Garden of Eden to dress it and to keep it. And the Lord God commanded the man, saying, Of every tree of the Garden thou mayest freely eat: But of the tree of the knowledge of good and evil, thou shalt not eat of it: for in the day that thou eatest thereof thou shalt surely die (Gen. 2:15–17).

When God spoke of death, He was not giving a threat, but a warning. Parents are not threatening their children when they warn them about a hot stove. If Adam chose not to love God enough to obey Him, he would die.

What is the record? What did Adam do? "And when the woman saw that the tree was good for food, and that it was pleasant to the eyes, and a tree to be desired to make one wise, she took of the fruit thereof, and did eat, and gave also unto her husband with her: and he did eat" (Gen. 3:6).

When Adam disobeyed God, he insulted his royal Guest. It is not that he committed murder or adultery, but that he failed to love and obey God which was his great sin. Adam was no longer a clean and holy house. He was now defiled by sin.

The sure and swift result of Adam's sin was death. God had said, "In the day that thou eateth thereof thou shalt surely die" (Gen. 2:17). But wait a minute! Did he surely die? The Bible records that Adam went on to live for many hundreds of years. Indeed he died, but it is so important to understand just how he died.

*He died immediately in the spirit.* Death in the biblical sense of the word is not primarily the separation of the soul from the body. For example, if I were to drop this pen and get very still and stay that way for a long time, some doctor might take my vital signs and say, "He is dead." But that would be inaccurate. I would simply have moved out of this body and gone on to heaven. Jesus said, "Whosoever liveth and believeth in me shall never die (John 11:26). So how could I be dead? I would be more alive than ever. And while you may attend my funeral, I'll be "kicking up gold-dust on the streets of Glory." For ". . . to be absent from the body, [is] to be present with the Lord" (2 Cor. 5:8).

Spiritual death is not the separation of the soul from the body but the separation of the spirit from God. Adam died spiritually that very day. What happened was that God's Holy Spirit moved out. God will not live in a dirty house. Adam came under what the Scripture calls the condemnation of sin and death.

A group of college boys wanted to keep the football team mascot, a goat, so they made intricate plans to smuggle the animal into their dormitory room.

"But what about the smell?" someone asked.

"The goat will just have to get used to it," the others replied.

College boys may be content to live in a dirty place, but a Holy God will not do so. It is against His very nature.

Now what was the result of God's moving out of Adam? God's Spirit is to the human spirit as blood is to the body. He is the life-giving power to the human spirit. John says, "In him was life; and the life was the light of men" (John 1:4). The Lord is the light and the life of man.

So when Adam sinned, the *Lord went out.* And when the Lord went out, the *life went out.* And when the life went out, the *light went out.* Now Adam had become spiritually depraved—no Lord. He was spiritually dead—no life. He was spiritually darkened—no light. In His death, burial, and resurrection centuries later, Jesus Christ would deal with all three matters.

*Adam died progressively in the soul.* His spirit was to receive directions from God's Spirit. "For as many as are led by the Spirit of God, they are the sons of God" (Rom. 8:14). Then Adam's spirit was in turn to give directions to Adam's soul (mind, emotion, and will), which would then motivate and direct Adam's body.

Man was not given the sense of instinct that most animals have. The reason for this is that God made available to him, instead, the Holy Spirit. He should be to man, in one sense, what instinct is to the other creatures. Can you imagine the confusion if instinct were removed from bees? Or from birds as they prepare to head south? Or from a guard dog as he senses danger? Take a look at what we call "civilization," and you will have some idea of the outcome!

So Adam is minus God in his spirit. God no longer lives in him and walks with him. He is no longer a spiritual man. He is now a natural man. That is, he is reduced to operating by his soul alone, because of sin. His spiritual transmitter is jammed. His mind has become a garden of weeds. His emotions begin to churn with fear. His will is corrupt and paralyzed. He is free to do as he wants, but not free to do as he ought.

Adam has now become master over his own house. Since God has moved out, his soul (mind, emotion, and will) has taken over the control center. Now he operates not as a God-centered man, but as a self-centered man.

Ever notice how a natural man operates? His mind says, "I think I want to do thus-and-so." His emotions say, "I feel like doing it." His will says, "All right, I'll do it." Do you know anybody who lives like that? The world is filled with such people. They are the living dead! It sounds like a horror movie, doesn't it? Well, it is horrible! "She that liveth in pleasure is dead while she liveth" (1 Tim. 5:6). Christians operate this way all too often.

*Adam died ultimately in his body.* "And all the days that Adam lived was 930 years: and he died" (Gen. 5:5).

Now, at last, his body has ceased to function. Adam, however, had been dead long before this. He was like a Christmas tree, cut off from the root (the transmitter of life) and brought into your living room. It looked good in your house with its colorful ornaments and lights. That is, it looked good until about New Year's Day! What happened when it was cut off gradually became obvious by outward deadness.

Similarly, many people, who are severed from God through sin, decorate themselves and even come to church on Sunday morning and try to worship. They may look very good, but somehow there's no life there. They may even try to please God, but they cannot pull it off. Many are aware that something is wrong, and they are miserable. They are cut off from the Source of true life, and ultimately they will die physically as well. As someone has said, that heartbeat under your shirt is but "a muffled drum beating a funeral march to the grave."

So God's first temple was Adam, but God moved out of Adam. And when God moved out, Adam died. Now Adam's death has been passed on to each of us. "Wherefore, as by one man sin entered into the world, and death by sin;

and so death passed upon all men, for that all have sinned" (Rom. 5:12). The Bible teaches that we all die in Adam.

But now comes the good part. Salvation is not merely getting man out of earth into heaven. It is also getting God out of heaven and back into man! Here's something exciting: When a person receives Christ and is born again, God puts into reverse the effects of sin. Adam died immediately in his spirit, progressively in his soul, and ultimately in his body. But when one becomes a child of God, he is *justified immediately* in his spirit, *sanctified progressively* in his soul, and *glorified ultimately* in his body.

Nearly two thousand years ago, God the Father made His final move to gain back His dwelling place among men. By the work of His Holy Spirit in the womb of a godly peasant woman, Mary, the eternal Son of God—the second person of the Trinity—assumed human flesh, became man, and was born on earth. Jesus Christ, from that miracle on, was and is fully God and fully man. They called His name Immanuel—God with us! As the firstborn of a whole new race—those with whom God dwells—Jesus Christ proved to us that God could inhabit humanity.

But this was not all. God's justice demands that our sin be dealt with. Jesus died to remove the sin barrier so that God can once more dwell in man. It was sin that caused God to move out, and He cannot return until that sin is properly dealt with. This, therefore, is the necessity of the cross.

If we were to choose one word that would describe the character of God above all other words, it would be "love," because God is love. In fact, He is perfect love. But let me suggest a word that perhaps epitomizes the character of God best: "holy." He is the thrice-holy God, for Isaiah tells us "Holy, holy, holy is the LORD of hosts" (Is. 6:3).

And because God is holy, His holiness demands that sin be properly judged. If God were to merely overlook our sin,

He would cease to be holy. In a court of law, it is said that when a guilty man is acquitted, the judge is condemned. God "will not at all acquit the wicked" (Nah. 1:3).

But hallelujah! Through faith in Christ's finished work at Calvary, we who believe are *immediately justified* in the spirit.

Now to him that worketh is the reward not reckoned of grace, but of debt. But to him that worketh not, but believeth on him that justifieth the ungodly, his faith is counted for righteousness. Even as David also describeth the blessedness of the man, unto whom God imputeth righteousness without works, Saying, Blessed are they whose iniquities are forgiven, and whose sins are covered. Blessed is the man to whom the Lord will not impute sin (Rom. 4:4–8).

God is free to move into the cleansed temple (our bodies) and to dwell in us because the barrier of sin has been taken away.

But not only are we justified in the spirit, now we can be *progressively sanctified* in the soul. The mind, emotion, and will can now be taken captive by the Holy Spirit within the human spirit, and we can begin to live like the persons we have become.

Remember that while justification is immediate, santification is a process. "Being confident of this very thing, that he which hath begun a good work in you will perform it until the day of Jesus Christ" (Phil. 1:6).

The old cowboy who was saved put it this way, "I ain't what I ought to be and I ain't what I'm goin' to be, but thank God I ain't what I was."

And one day we will be *ultimately glorified* in our bodies. Every Christian should be looking for the coming of the Lord Jesus, who "shall change our vile body, that it may be fashioned like unto his glorious body, according to the working whereby he is able even to subdue all things under himself" (Phil. 3:21).

Therefore, it is not until the resurrection that our salvation will be complete. It is really in three stages:

*Past tense.* I have been justified in my spirit and have been saved from the penalty of sin.

*Present tense.* I am being sanctified in my soul and am being saved from the power of sin.

*Future tense.* I will be glorified in my body and will be saved from the possibility of sin.

But until the time of my glorification, I have a royal Resident who lives in me and has promised He will never leave nor forsake me.

# When Glory
# Fills the House

*And it came to pass, when the priests were come out of the holy place, that the cloud filled the house of the LORD, So that the priests could not stand to minister because of the cloud: for the glory of the LORD had filled the house of the LORD (1 Kin. 8:10,11).*

*And be not drunk with wine, wherein is excess; but be filled with the Spirit (Eph. 5:18).*

When King Solomon dedicated that magnificent temple on Mount Moriah, it was, among other things, an object-lesson, an illustration of every believer in the Lord Jesus Christ. For now, after Pentecost, at the moment of our salvation, we become temples of the Holy Spirit. God through His Holy Spirit indwells us just as His Spirit with shekinah glory came and filled the holy of holies of Solomon's temple when it was fully dedicated to Him.

Yet some Christians appear not to be filled with the Holy Spirit. Glory does not fill their house. They have allowed the self-life and the cares of this world to move the Lord Jesus from that place of preeminence that is rightfully His. They are no longer Spirit-filled, but carnal. Therefore, we have the admonition of the apostle Paul, "And be not drunk with wine, wherein is excess; but be filled with the Spirit" (Eph. 5:18).

In this chapter we are going to address the matter of the Spirit-filled life. But I wish here to emphasize that a Spirit-filled Christian is not some super-edition of a Christian. He is not a regular believer raised to the highest power! For all normal Christians are to be experiencing the Spirit-filled life. This is not some special touch for the evangelist or minister, but this fullness is for every blood-bought child of God. "For the promise is unto you, and to your children, and to all that are afar off, even as many as the Lord our God shall call" (Acts 2:39).

Paul, in Ephesians 5 and 6, gives the reasons, the requirements, and the results of this Spirit-filled life.

## Reasons for the Spirit-filled Life

The first reason for any Christian to be Spirit-filled is simple *obedience.* God has command us "be filled with the Spirit." This is not a suggestion nor a request, but a command. The Christian who is not Spirit-filled is really living in rebellion. His disobedience to God is not weakness, but wickedness.

Any congregation would be scandalized should the minister attempt to preach a sermon while drunk. His thick tongue, bleary eyes, and foolish thoughts would cause a quick meeting of the elders, deacons, or other official bodies within the church. What a disgraceful thing it would be. How tongues would wag!

Yet I sincerely believe it would be a greater sin for any man of God to fail to be filled with the Spirit when preaching than to be drunk. The same verse that commands us not to be "drunk with wine" commands us to be "filled with the Spirit." The Scripture also teaches that sins of omission are greater than sins of commission. Therefore, it is a greater sin to fail to do what we ought to do than to do what we ought not to do. As a matter of fact, if we are doing what we ought to do, we cannot be doing what we ought not to do.

Now I am not minimizing the sin of drunkenness. But in my estimation, the cause of Christ has been hurt far more by Christians who were carnal and not Spirit-filled than by Christians who were drunk. I have known of churches that have been torn apart by carnal leadership. Many people who are at the forefront of church splits are teetotallers. The devil would rather start a fuss in the body of Christ than to sell a barrel of whiskey any day.

It is important for us to understand that the Spirit-filled life is not some option. It is not merely a blessing to enjoy. It is a command to obey. To fail to obey is a sin worse than being drunk.

A second reason that Paul gives for being filled with the Spirit is our *obligation*. Christians have tremendous responsibilities that they must fulfill.

*Look at the obligation of our worship life.* "Speaking to yourselves in psalms and hymns and spiritual songs, singing and making melody in your heart to the Lord" (Eph. 5:19). Our worship life is to be alive with joy and the reality of Christ. This kind of worship is the overflow of the Spirit-filled life. It is what Jesus called "worship in spirit" (John 4:24 NIV). Yet many Christians would confess that for them worship could be more aptly described with these words, "How tedious and tasteless the hours."

*Look at the obligation of our wedded life.* "Wives, submit yourselves unto your own husbands, as unto the Lord" (Eph. 5:22). This verse teaches that a Christian wife is to submit to her husband as to Christ. In this day of the feminist movement, the role of the submitted wife is doubly difficult. You need to know such submission is not popular, and it has never been done in any age apart from the power of the Holy Spirit.

Incidentally, submission does not mean the woman is inferior. Everyone knows that a woman is infinitely superior to a man—at being a woman! And the man is infinitely superior to a woman—at being a man. God made us different so that He might make us one.

It is Satan's idea that submission means inferiority. I like to think of Eden as a three-act tragedy—Adam's rib, Satan's fib, and women's lib. A woman is truly liberated by the Spirit of God when she is freed not only to do what she wants, but to do what she ought. And God says she ought to obey her husband to find freedom.

And the husband is to love his wife as Christ loved the church. "Husbands, love your wives, even as Christ also loved the church, and gave himself for it" (Eph. 5:25). How does Jesus love the church? He loves it sacrificially and completely. A husband should be willing to die for his wife, but he need not die physically to live sacrificially for her.

And men, note that far more is required of the husband than of the wife. The wife's model is the church, but the husband's is Christ Himself. How is any mortal man going to do anything as Jesus does it? There is no way apart from the Spirit-filled life.

*Look at the obligation of our work life.* "Servants, be obedient to them that are your masters according to the flesh, with fear and trembling, in singleness of your heart, as unto Christ; Not with eye-service, as menpleasers; but as the servants of Christ, doing the will of God from the heart" (Eph. 6:5,6). These verses teach that we should work for our employers as though they were the Lord Jesus Christ. Paul says, "as unto Christ."

When a man goes to the employment agency looking for new workers, he ought to say, "If you have any Christians, please give them the first opportunity. I don't understand it, but they are different from my other workers. They are on time; they do not gossip, cheat, or steal. They work hard. You would think that they think I am the Lord."

I am convinced that if employees began to live like that on Monday far more employers would believe what is preached on Sunday.

*Look at the obligation of our war life.* "For we wrestle not against flesh and blood, but against principalities, against powers, against the rulers of the darkness of this world, against spiritual wickedness in high places" (Eph. 6:12). The Christian is at war! Ours is a fight to the finish with a sinister foe, and there are no holds barred. Satan is our adversary and he has let loose with all of the artillery of hell. We will never defeat him with human flesh. If the battle were against mere humanity, then flesh might defeat flesh. But this is a spiritual war. Satan laughs at our organizations, mocks at our schemes, but he trembles before the mighty power of God released through a Spirit-filled saint. I pity the Christian soldier who fights Satan with his own puny human strength.

A third reason for being filled with the Spirit is our *opportunities.* "Redeeming the time, because the days are evil. Wherefore be ye not unwise, but understanding what the will of the Lord is" (Eph. 5:16,17). These verses come just before the command to be filled. It is God's reminder that we are to use our time and opportunity wisely. Any day that is not crowned with the Christian being consciously and conspicuously filled with the Holy Spirit is a wasted day. It will be lost for all eternity. At the judgment seat of Christ, it will at best be counted as wood, hay, and stubble.

Oh, what golden opportunities we let slip through our fingers because the Spirit is not in control. There has never been a greater day or age to witness for Christ than ours. There is such a need and such a hunger everywhere.

But I have noticed that there is a subtle but deadly thing happening in the lives of some Christians. They see the

Spirit-filled life simply as a source of enjoyment rather than a force for employment. They are interested in spiritual gifts, but they think of spiritual gifts as toys rather than tools.

A woman was giving a word of appreciation to her first-aid class. She said, "There was a terrible accident in front of my house. A man was lying there with bones splintered, rolling around in pools of blood. His arteries were severed. He was in a state of shock. But I remembered my first-aid instructions that if I would put my head between my knees, I wouldn't faint. It worked and I didn't faint. I am so grateful that I took this class."

Some Christians are like that. We need to get our heads from between our knees and realize that Jesus said, "But ye shall receive power, after that the Holy Ghost is come upon you: and ye shall be witnesses unto me both in Jerusalem, and in all Judea, and in Samaria, and unto the uttermost part of the earth" (Acts 1:8). We are filled with the Holy Spirit to "Rescue the perishing,/Care for the dying,/. . . Tell them of Jesus, the mighty to save." Our opportunities are a reason to be Spirit-filled.

## Requirements for the Spirit-filled Life

How indeed does the Holy Spirit fill us? In answering this question, it should be noted that the Holy Spirit is a Person, as God the Father and God the Son are Persons. He acts, wills, loves, and may be grieved or insulted. I say this because some people think of the Holy Spirit as some kind of impersonal force or power emanating from God.

The Holy Spirit does indeed have force and power, but He is a Person. So the concept of being filled with the Holy Spirit is not that of a vessel being filled by some substance or a machine being supercharged with power, but of a human house being completely occupied by a divine Person. We are not commingled with God; we are still human, and He is forever divine. But we are empowered by Him, used by Him.

With that concept in mind, let me mention three requirements for the Spirit-filled life.

*There must be complete commitment to the Spirit.* We all have had guests in our homes. We double up the kids in one room and make a place for the newcomers. We clear the space in the closet for their clothes. "Here's your room. Here's the bath. Here are the extra towels. Here's the refrigerator and a key to the house. Make yourself at home. Our house is your house," we say.

But suppose you come home one day to find your guest in your own bedroom going through your personal records. He is reading your old love letters, your tax reports, and your personal will. You clear your throat and try to be calm as you ask, "Are you looking for something that I can help you with?" But by the tone of your voice you are really asking, "What are you doing here? You have no business in my personal papers!"

Your guest replies, "No, thank you; I don't need any help. I was just curious about your personal affairs and thought these things would be interesting reading."

By this time you cannot control your anger. "You have no business prying into my personal papers. That desk should not concern you. Please leave it immediately."

Your guest responds, "I don't understand you. You said that I was to make myself at home. This house was my house."

"Well, I didn't mean that you are to pry into my personal affairs."

And a friendship begins to unravel.

Have you ever been guilty of doing something like that to the Holy Spirit? "Dear Holy Spirit, come and live in the temple of my body. My heart is your abode. Make yourself completely at home." But the searching question is: Have you given Him the key to every room, every closet, every desk? Is there any part of your life that is off limits to your heavenly Guest? If so, you are not filled with the Spirit.

The Holy Spirit must have the key to your business life, your social life, your thought life. The Holy Spirit deserves and demands access to every corner of the temple that Christ purchased with His blood. "What? . . . know ye not that your body is the temple of the Holy Ghost which is in you, which ye have of God, and ye are not your own?" (1 Cor. 6:19). He will not settle for a place—even of prominence. He demands preeminence.

Years ago some ministers were planning a united evangelistic crusade. They met to select an evangelist. The majority wanted D. L. Moody, an evangelist who was filled with the Spirit and anointed with God's mighty power to preach His Word.

One minister on the committee, however, was holding out for another evangelist. In exasperation he said, "Moody, Moody, Moody. That is the only name you seem to know. Does Moody have a monopoly on the Holy Spirit?"

One of the others answered and said, "No, but it seems that the Holy Spirit has a monopoly on Moody."

That's what I'm talking about. Does the Holy Spirit have a monopoly on you? Have you given Him the key to every room? Is He merely resident or is He president? Have you made a complete commitment to Him?

*There will be continual control by the Spirit.* Ephesians 5:18 actually may be translated, *"Be ye being filled* with the Spirit." This matter of the Spirit-filled life is not a once-for-all matter. To be sure, there may be a crisis experience when we yield our all to Him, but this crisis is followed by a process. The Holy Spirit must be recognized day-by-day as we yield to Him.

48

We said a few pages back that the command is "be not drunk with wine . . . but be filled with the Spirit." Why didn't the Lord say, "Don't commit adultery but be filled with the Spirit?" Or why didn't He name lying, stealing, pride, or some other sin in contrast to being Spirit-filled?

The answer is that not only is He speaking by way of contrast, but He is also speaking by comparison. There is a sense in which the result of being Spirit-filled may be compared to being intoxicated. The disciples were accused of being drunk with new wine when they were filled with the Spirit on the day of Pentecost. Peter answered and said, "They are not drunk as you suppose" (Acts 2:15, paraphrased). Interestingly enough, he did not deny that they were drunk. He just said, "They are not drunk *as you suppose* (italics mine).

When a man is drunk, he is brought under control by another power. Liquor has been called "the devil in liquid form." Satan takes over a man's life: his walk, his talk, his thoughts, his courage, his morals all change for the worse. But when a man is Spirit-filled, they are changed for the better.

And here is the point. How does a man get drunk? He drinks! But how does he stay drunk? He must keep drinking. I believe I know some Christians who have once been Spirit-filled but they have "sobered up." As Christians, we must keep drinking from that fountain that never shall run dry.

In order for there to be continual control, there must be continual appropriation of the dear Holy Spirit in all of His fullness. Remember that He is a Person and not a substance, like wine; but as we yield to Him totally, He affects the whole personality.

*There must be a conscious claiming of the Spirit.* At the close of a previous chapter, I urged you to let the Holy Spirit assume control of your life. Remember that when the Holy

Spirit came in, He came in as a divine person. It is so easy to miss what Paul is saying. He does not say to be filled *by* the Spirit but *with* the Spirit. We must not get the idea that the Holy Spirit is waiting outside of us to place into us what we need.

If that were so, we might say, "I need more love," and He would fill us with love. Or, "I need more patience," and He pours in the patience. But that is not the idea at all. That would be being filled by the Spirit. We are to be filled *with* the Spirit.

He floods every area of our lives with His blessed self. Therefore, when He is there, we have all that we can ever need. He is love, patience, and everything else that we could ever need. In Him, we are complete.

A pastor's wife was at her wit's end. She was left alone near the small country church her husband pastored with two active children while her husband commuted to the seminary for his weekday studies. The pressures that were upon her were terrific, and she cried out to God for help. "Give me more patience, Lord. Give me more strength, Lord. Give me more love, Lord." Yet she had no victory.

One day it dawned upon her that through the Holy Spirit, Jesus was alive and well and living within the temple of her body. Her prayers began to change. She no longer prayed, "Give me more patience, Lord." Now her prayer was, "Thy patience, Lord."

She made a conscious claiming of that which was already hers. *All that she needed she already had.* She recognized the presence and gracious sufficiency of the Holy Spirit in her. Every need was just waiting to be claimed by faith. Immediately there was a new release of power as God's Holy Spirit expressed His love, patience, and strength. The difference was dramatic.

## Results of the Spirit-filled Life

The verses that follow the command to be filled with the Spirit in Ephesians 5 speak of the results that are sure to manifest themselves when the Lord Jesus Christ is enthroned in the holy temple of our bodies.

*In our relationship to God, there will be a spirit of adoration.* "Speaking to yourselves in psalms and hymns and spiritual songs, singing and making melody in your heart to the Lord" (Eph. 5:19). As we have already noted, it is the holy obligation of the people of God and the blessed privilege of the church to worship the Lord God in the Spirit.

As our means of adoration, Paul speaks of psalms and hymns and spiritual songs. The Old Testament psalms were the song book both of Israel and of the early church. Hymns and songs of praise issue forth adoration directly to God. Spiritual songs seem to mean joyful and spontaneous music that overflows from the heart.

The whole idea is that Spirit-filled worship, whether congregational or personal, joyfully comes from the heart and is to be unto the Lord.

It seems almost a truism to repeat that songs of worship should be sung "to the Lord." Yet it definitely needs to be said. Much music today in our churches is not real worship at all, but flesh on parade. Just as we may pray to be "seen of men" (Matt. 6:5) we can sing the same way. We are often singing one to another rather than to the Lord.

Perhaps the worse thing that could be said about some music is not that it is off key, but rather that it is sung to the wrong audience. I have observed that when music is truly sung to the Lord, it does speak to the congregation also.

I am also convinced that God is not all that impressed

with musical perfection. None of us should ever do less than is best musically, but for some of us our best is not so great. One minister of music called me a "prisoner-singer." He said, "You are always behind a few bars and can't find the right key."

Be that as it may, God had just as soon hear a blackbird sing as a nightingale, and I am convinced that He is pleased when I make melody in my heart. Really, the phrase "making melody" means to strum an instrument. Therefore I am to make music not *in* my heart, but *with* my heart. My heart is to be the instrument of praise for God's glory.

*In our relationship to circumstances, there will be a spirit of appreciation.* "Giving thanks always for all things unto God and the Father in the name of our Lord Jesus Christ" (Eph. 5:20).

Perhaps the most common but often-transgressed command in the Bible is the command to be thankful. A carnal Christian is often grumbly hateful. The Spirit-filled Christian is humbly grateful.

This command to be thankful would not be such a difficult one had the Lord not said "always" and "all things."

> *We thank Him for sun,*
> *Do we thank Him for rain?*
> *We thank Him for joy,*
> *Do we thank Him for pain?*
> *We thank Him for gains,*
> *Do we thank Him for losses?*
> *We thank Him for blessings,*
> *Do we thank Him for crosses?*

To give thanks when things go wrong, when there is personal hurt, cancer, divorce, financial reverse, or heartbreaking disappointment seems so unnatural. But when we give thanks, we are not necessarily expressing approval of those things for which we give thanks. We are rather announcing our faith that our God is greater than any of these items.

Since God is love and God is sovereign, there is no area where He does not rule or overrule. Nothing comes to us unless He allows it. Not a blade of grass moves without His permission. Romans 8:28 is always true. "And we know that all things work together for good to them that love God, to them who are the called according to his purpose." Therefore we can give thanks.

*In our relationship to others, there will be a spirit of accommodation.* "Submitting yourselves one to another in the fear of God" (Eph. 5:21).

When a person insists on "standing up for his rights," he most likely knows little of the Spirit-filled life. We have been crucified with Christ. What rights does a dead man have? "What? . . . know ye not that your body is the temple of the Holy Ghost which is in you, which ye have of God, and *ye are not your own?* (1 Cor. 6:19, italics mine.)

Submission is one equal willingly and lovingly placing himself under another equal that Jesus may be glorified. "For we preach not ourselves, but Christ Jesus the Lord; and ourselves your servants for Jesus' sake" (2 Cor. 4:5).

We do not submit to one another because of one another as such but because of the Lord Jesus Christ. And submission, therefore, is not just for women. It is for Christians!

The Spirit-filled life is for all of us who know Jesus Christ. Why settle for anything less than God's best for you? And remember, it is not your job to persuade Him to fill you, but to permit Him to do so when you give Him every key to the rooms in your house. Don't ever be content with anything less!

# Doing What Comes Supernaturally

*But the natural man receiveth not the things of the Spirit of God: for they are foolishness unto him: neither can he know them, because they are spiritually discerned (1 Cor. 2:14).*

*But he that is spiritual judgeth all things, yet he himself is judged of no man (1 Cor. 2:15).*

*And I, brethren, could not speak unto you as unto spiritual, but as unto carnal, even as unto babes in Christ (1 Cor. 3:1).*

The noted Southern Baptist preacher, the late Dr. Robert G. Lee, once preached an excoriating sermon against sin. He didn't pull any punches. A lady whose feathers had been ruffled met him at the door and said, "I didn't appreciate that sermon one little bit."

Dr. Lee reportedly replied, "The devil didn't either. So classify yourself."

Classification is not always flattering, but it is always needed in spiritual matters. The Bible teaches that, in the broad sense, there are three categories or classes of persons living on planet earth. In the Scriptures these are called *the natural man,* *the spiritual man,* and *the carnal man.*

Classification is important to us because it is the starting point in our understanding of the journey of faith. One cannot get to where he ought to be until he recognizes where he is. The Bible is God's road map to maturity. But many a confused traveler has discovered that a map is of very little use in getting us where we ought to be until we first discover where we are.

So as we study the characteristics of the natural man, the spiritual man, and the carnal man, may God show us where we are and help us to get where we need to be.

First meet the natural man, who is

## Doing What Comes Naturally

Why do we call the natural man by such a term? Because he is just that—natural. He is the sum total of what he has received by nature from his first birth.

*He is born into the natural world.* He may have been born well physically, but because he has not been born again, he is not a part of the spiritual world.

Because he has had no second birth, he is dead to the spiritual world. He may have received many admirable traits through his natural birth. He may grow to be witty, charming, cultured, outwardly moral, educated, and religious: Still, having been born only once, he is spiritually dead. Naturally!

The Scripture says, "In Adam all die" (1 Cor. 15:22). What does that mean? Let us do a quick review.

Remember that Adam was designed to be a house inhabited by the Lord. God's Holy Spirit was to indwell and give life to Adam's human spirit. But when Adam sinned, he died. He did not die an immediate physical death, but he did die spiritually at that moment. We said that spiritual death is the separation of the Spirit of God from the spirit of man. God moved out of Adam's spirit. Adam became devoid of God in the spirit.

Concerning our Lord Jesus, God says by contrast, "In him

was life; and the life was the light of men" (John 1:4). So when the Lord went out of Adam, the life went out, and the light went out.

Now how does this apply to us? Every person born since that time has inherited Adam's nature. We are born minus God in the spirit—dead, depraved, and darkened like our father Adam.

Thus, when we say that man was made in the image of God, we need to remember it is Adam to whom we are referring. That image was marred and defaced by sin. The Bible says, concerning Adam's children, "And Adam lived a hundred and thirty years, and begat a son in his own likeness, after his image; and called his name Seth" (Gen. 5:3).

We are born, therefore, in the image of Adam rather than in the image of God. Incidentally, that is a comforting thought. I would hate to look around at humanity as it is and think that we are all in the image of God. Surely God is in better shape than that!

This deadness to spiritual things that we inherited from Adam does not mean that every person is outwardly vile or inwardly cruel. One person's lifestyle may not be as corrupt as someone who is more wicked. But both are just as dead. When a body is dead in the physical realm, there may be degrees of corruption and decay, but there are not degrees of deadness. Dead is dead! All people in Adam are from the same mold, but I will agree that some may be moldier than others.

*He is blind to the spiritual world.* Because of this deadness and darkness, the natural man has no appreciation of spiritual things. Look again at Paul's words. "But the natural man receiveth not the things of the Spirit of God: for they are foolishness unto him: neither can he know them, because they are spiritually discerned" (1 Cor. 2:14). The word "receiveth" here means to welcome as one would welcome a house guest. The natural man, therefore, has no welcome for Christ or for the things of God.

We need to be clear in our understanding here. This does not necessarily mean the natural man may not enjoy coming to a religious service. He may thrill at the great music. His aesthetic nature can appreciate sunlight streaming through a stained-glass window. The natural man can be stirred by the oratory of a gifted pastor. He may receive great comfort from the warm handshake of friendly people who congregate together. Yet he does not truly welcome the message of God to his spirit. He does not surrender to Christ. Satan knows this and therefore is not against religion as such. He would just as soon send a man to hell from the pew as from the gutter.

Paul amplifies this lack of appreciation of the natural man for spiritual things when he says, "For the preaching of the cross is to them that perish foolishness; but unto us which are saved it is the power of God" (1 Cor. 1:18). The natural man does not know the real meaning of the cross that is at the heart of our faith.

Even if he could get there in his natural state, heaven would become a form of hell for the natural man. There are some people who think they want to live forever who don't even know what to do on a rainy afternoon. What would a person with no appreciation for the things of God do in heaven for all eternity?

Not only does the natural man have no appreciation for spiritual things, he has no comprehension of them, ". . . neither can he know them, because they are spiritually discerned" (1 Cor. 2:14).

What good is a television set if the tuner is broken? No program could be received. The natural man has no spiritual apparatus, as it were, to receive divine impulses. Oh, he may hear the words, but he never really gets the message.

Nicodemus was an educated man. He was a ruler in Israel. Jesus told him one night that he had to be born again before he could see or perceive the kingdom of heaven (John 3:3).

When I talk with a natural man about Jesus Christ and he says, "I just don't see it that way," I don't argue with him. Why scold a blind man for not seeing? Our job is to bear witness to Christ, then pray that God in mercy will turn the light of His revelation onto the darkened spirit of the person involved.

*He is bound to this material world.* To compound the tragedy of life without God, because the natural man has no appreciation for the spiritual world, he lives basically for the same things that an animal lives for—self-gratification, self-preservation, and self-propagation. He cannot rise above the material and animalistic level of living without the miracle of a birth from above.

Whenever I meet a natural man, my heart yearns to say, "There is more, so much more!"

The second category is the spiritual man. He is

## Doing What Comes Supernaturally

What are the marks of the spiritual man who is living a supernatural life?

*The spiritual man lives by the Spirit.* "Now we have received, not the spirit of the world, but the spirit which is of God; that we might know the things that are freely given to us of God" (1 Cor. 2:12).

He that is spiritual is simply he who has received the Spirit of God. Because of that he has received life. He has been born from above. He is not merely a natural man who has been improved. He is not like a tadpole who has finally turned into a frog. He is more like a frog who has been transformed into a prince by the kiss of God's grace. Christians are not merely nice characters. They are new creatures.

We must remember, too, that salvation is a matter of receiving Christ through His Spirit into our hearts. It is not merely getting one's sins forgiven. Forgiveness is necessary, but it just sets the stage for salvation. Nor is salvation merely going to heaven when one dies. That is wonderful, but it is the by-product of salvation.

Salvation begins with getting the Lord, the life, and the light back into the deadened spirit of man.

*The spiritual man learns from the Spirit.*

Now we have received, not the spirit of the world, but the spirit which is of God; that we might know the things that are freely given to us of God. Which things also we speak, not in the words which man's wisdom teacheth, but which the Holy Ghost teacheth; comparing spiritual things with spiritual. But the natural man receiveth not the things of the Spirit of God: for they are foolishness unto him: neither can he know them, because they are spiritually discerned (1 Cor. 2:12–14).

"We have received the Spirit . . . that we may know," Paul says. There are some things that can only be known through the illumination of the Holy Spirit. The human spirit becomes the organ of spiritual knowledge. The Lord reveals spiritual truth to the human spirit. Of course, the mind and the emotions come into play, but they depend on that revelation which the human spirit has received from the Lord.

The One who brings God's truth to the human spirit is the Holy Spirit. I must always keep this in my mind and heart when I preach. How important it is that I depend upon Him. For while I can preach truth, only the Holy Spirit can impart truth. An intellectual pursuit of the Bible is important. But remember, the mind can only help us to understand what God has revealed to us by His Spirit.

When God wants to illumine man, the lamp He uses is the human spirit. But the oil that feeds that lamp is the Holy

Spirit. How wise we would be if we would learn to burn the oil of divine illumination rather than the wick of human intuition, which quickly burns out and leaves so much smoke.

*The spiritual man is liberated through the Spirit.* "But he that is spiritual judgeth all things, yet he himself is judged of no man. For who hath known the mind of the Lord, that he may instruct Him? But we have the mind of Christ" (1 Cor. 2:15,16).

How is the spiritual man liberated? He is no longer chained to the chariot wheels of this world's system. He sees right through it. He judges, or discerns, all things. The word "judges" is a legal word that implies an examination upon the basis of illuminated insight and knowledge.

Because of the Holy Spirit, the value system of the spiritual man is operating aright. He is set free from the bondage that has enslaved the thinking of the natural man. This truth sets the spiritual man free.

First Corinthians 2:16 continues, "Yet he himself is judged of no man." That means that the spiritual man will forever be a puzzle to the world. The things that motivate the natural man do not motivate the spiritual man. He marches to the beat of a different drummer.

Don't feel, however, that the spiritual man is going to be an oddity. He is not odd—just different. Whatever is odd about a Christian was probably odd about him before he got converted. Yet there will be an exciting distinctiveness that marks the liberated saint. The world will be puzzled at the victory that is ours.

There is yet a third kind of person that Paul mentions. This is not the natural man, nor the spiritual man. He once had been spiritual but is now known as carnal (fleshly), and he is

## Doing What Comes Unnaturally

And why do we say he is unnatural? Because he is a strange mixture. He is neither fish nor fowl. He has truly been saved, for Paul calls these carnal believers "brethren," and yet, he looks and acts much like an unsaved person. What are the marks of carnality that Paul mentions?

*The carnal Christian is deformed.* "And I, brethren, could not speak unto you as unto spiritual, but as unto carnal, even as unto babes in Christ" (1 Cor. 3:1).

Paul says the carnal Christian is like a baby who has never grown up. There is a legitimate babyhood (and who doesn't love a baby?). What a delight came into our home when God sent each of our babies. But think of the grief that would have been ours if after many years our children were still acting like babies. It was a thrill when they first said, "Da, da." But if my twenty-one-year-old son were to speak that way to me today, there would be no amusement at all.

Now in the realm of the physical, when a child has not developed, the parents do not judge or condemn that child if there are physical reasons. They only pour more love and care into that precious life.

But it is quite another matter when, for no reason at all, we do not develop and grow. How sad in the spiritual realm when we have all that we need to grow, and yet, because of stubbornness, ignorance, laziness, and sin we are the spiritual counterpart of a gray-headed baby. We are spiritually deformed. It is one thing to be childlike. It is quite another thing to be childish.

*The carnal Christian is dependent.* "I have fed you with milk, and not with meat: for hitherto ye were not able to bear it, neither yet now are ye able" (1 Cor. 3:2).

Paul says that, like a little baby, the carnal Christian must be fed with a milk diet. There is nothing wrong with a milk diet for the newborn, but oh, there are so many more good things to taste and enjoy for the adult.

Milk is technically predigested food. Carnal Christians expect a pastor to bottle feed them on Sundays and then burp them on their way out of the sanctuary.

Because of his weak digestion and spiritual dependency, the carnal Christian never gets in theology much beyond "hell is hot, heaven is sweet, and Jesus saves." Thank God that these things are true, but there is so much more to know and enjoy about the Lord Jesus Christ. While the spiritual man is sitting down to a juicy, spiritual steak with all the trimmings, the carnal Christian never gets beyond his milk, pabulum, and strained beets. And he even needs someone to feed him those.

*The carnal Christian is divisive.* "For ye are yet carnal: for whereas there is among you envying, and strife, and divisions, are ye not carnal, and walk as men?" (1 Cor. 3:3).

Like a spoiled brat, the carnal Christian is often the center of division and controversy in the church. I have noticed that little children are hardly ever concerned about the great issues of life. They are more apt to pout if the toast is cut straight across rather than diagonally so it will look like a little sailboat. In the church, there are big babies who really never are concerned about the greater matters of our faith but who can become absolutely unbending over which side of the auditorium the organ should be placed.

In the Corinthian church, they had gotten into petty squabbles over personalities. They had their favorite-preacher syndrome. Some were in the Paul camp. "He is such a great theologian." Some were in the Peter camp. "He tells it like it is." Others were followers of Apollos. "Did you ever hear such oratory?"

Here are Paul's words to these big babies. "Therefore let no man glory in men. For all things are yours; Whether Paul, or Apollos, or Cephas, or the world, or life, or death, or things present, or things to come; all are yours; And ye are Christ's; and Christ is God's" (1 Cor. 3:21–23).

Thus we have God's "classified section" of spiritual life. It's not there to put us down, but to urge us on. For when we know where we are, then by God's grace, we can begin to move to where we ought to be.

Let the natural man repent from his sins and receive Christ. Let the carnal man repent of his sins and enthrone Christ. Let the spiritual man keep on repenting when he sins and grow on and on to greater maturity and enjoyment of Christ.

# Inhabited
# or Inhibited?

*For ye see your calling, brethren, how that not many wise men after the flesh, not many mighty, not many noble, are called; But God hath chosen the foolish things of the world to confound the wise; and God hath chosen the weak things of the world to confound the things which are mighty; And base things of the world, and things which are despised, hath God chosen, yea, and things which are not, to bring to nought things that are (1 Cor. 1:26–28).*

Let's see just who is reading this chapter. May I ask you a few questions about yourself? Are you a Phi Beta Kappa, an All-American, Miss America, listed in *Who's Who*, voted Most Likely to Succeed or in the *Bluebook* of society? If you answered yes to any of these or to all of these, I've got good news for you. God can use you, too, but He is going to have a little more difficulty in doing it.

But if, on the other hand, you have done or achieved none of the things the world so highly prizes, God still wants to use you. If you never won anything but the booby prize, God will delight to get glory through you. As a matter of fact, He would rather use ordinary people.

But there is one thing to avoid. Many Christians are going around with an inferiority complex that is an insult to the mighty God who inhabits their hearts. They stand sometimes with drooping shoulders and apologetic voice and declare, "I just serve God in my poor, little, weak way." I want to say, "Well, quit it! He doesn't want you to serve Him that way. He wants you to serve Him in His mighty, dynamic way. You are a temple of God. It is there that His glory is to be displayed!" What some people call humility, I call poor posture.

You see, God has a wonderful plan. He is in the business of getting glory to Himself, and here is how He does it. He takes what the world calls a foolish message. "For the preaching of the cross is to them that perish foolishness; but unto us who are saved it is the power of God" (1 Cor. 1:18). He then chooses what the world considers to be a weak and unworthy messenger and compounds the two in the crucible of His own mighty power and wisdom, and the result is glory to God.

God does it this way, "That no flesh should glory in His presence" (1 Cor. 1:29).

## Embarrassing Qualifications

To serve God in this mighty army of the ordinary, there are some downright embarrassing qualifications. Let's see how close we come to being admissible.

*The foolish ones.* The word "foolish" that Paul mentions in the above Scripture comes from the Greek word *moros*. It is the word from which our word "moron" comes. It denotes someone who is dull, sluggish, or perhaps even somewhat silly.

So you were not at the top of your class? You hold no Ph.D.? Does this mean that you cannot be used? To the contrary. God is looking for someone just like you. Relationship is more important than scholarship.

*The weak ones.* The word Paul used for weak means physical weakness, even infirmity. Are you feeling weak and sickly? Congratulations! God is willing to do mighty things with and through your frail body. His strength will be made perfect in your weakness.

*The base ones.* This word that Paul used means of low birth, ignoble, without pedigree. Perhaps you are not from the aristocracy. You were not born with a silver spoon in your mouth. You may be like a seminary classmate of mine who said, "I wasn't born in a log cabin like some of the great men of our country, but I want you to know that just as soon as our family could afford one, we bought it and moved in!" Praise God, He delights to use those who were born on the wrong side of the tracks. Don't let your social inferiority keep you from serving Him.

*The despised ones.* This word means those that the world writes off as no account. It means those who are treated with contempt and scorn. Are there those who look down on you, and say you will never amount to anything? That is terrific! That means that when God does use you, it will be obvious to all around that He is the One who is doing it and He, therefore, will get the glory.

*The ones who are not.* This refers to people who are completely overlooked. They do not even get to be despised. They are not considered enough to be despised. They are not listed in *Who's Who.* They are not even listed in *Who's Not.*

Am I by chance talking about you? Your name is never listed in the church bulletin? When people stand around, your name is not discussed, either for good or evil? Do you consider yourself a nobody? Well, with God everybody is a somebody. He is looking for someone like you. Your name may not be mentioned much down here, but God wants you to make headlines in heaven.

Now let me make three things clear concerning God's plan to use His ordinary people:

First, God does not say not *any* mighty, not *any* noble are called. But He does say, not *many* . . . I thank God for the wealthy, the gifted, the intellectuals who know and serve the Lord Jesus Christ.

Indeed Paul was one of these. This gifted religious aristocrat had one of the most scintillating minds of all of the ages. He was sought after, flattered, and praised by his peers. He achieved the highest positions in the religious world and had an academic pedigree that was impeccable. Yet, Paul said, concerning these achievements, "I . . . count them but dung, that I may win Christ" (Phil. 3:8).

The second thing that I emphasize as we talk about qualifications is this: Paul is not encouraging half-heartedness, laziness, or mediocrity.

If you are a preacher with only an average IQ, you must study all the more. A preacher in Pennsylvania was noted as an expert fox hunter. An old Quaker said to him one day, "If I were a fox, I would hide me where thee could not find me."

"And where is that?" inquired the preacher.

"In thy study!" the Quaker replied.

You may be a singer with less than a great voice, but still it ought to be your ambition to make that voice sing the sweetest note it can sing for the glory of the Lord Jesus Christ.

You may not have great physical strength. You may not have mountains of muscle and bulging biceps, but the important thing is that every nerve, fiber, bone, and sinew in your body be given over completely to the Lord Jesus. Let Him have every ounce and every inch. It has well been said, "It doesn't take much of a man to be a Christian—just all there is of him."

Thirdly, remember that Paul is not talking about relying upon our own strength anyway. The secret of the whole matter is that God gives to ordinary people extraordinary power. Remember that He gave Himself *for us* in order that He might give Himself *to us* and, therefore, live His life *through us*. It is not so much our responsibility as it is our response to His ability.

## God's Mighty Weak Ones

When I think of God using "foolish" things, I think of Billy Sunday. He was the best-known evangelist of his day. In many ways he was his day's counterpart to Billy Graham.

He certainly could not be classed as an intellectual. He only had a high school education. He used slang language and had some laughable ideas. His antics on the preaching platform scandalized some of the more refined church members of that era. One biographer called him "God's laugh at the preachers."

One of my older seminary professors told me of his going to hear Billy Sunday preach when the evangelist was in his heyday. He said that Billy carried on and performed in his usual way, but then God moved on him and he struck fire. He began to preach "hell hot, heaven sweet, judgment sure, and Jesus saves!" He then gave the invitation to "hit the sawdust trail," and here they came—multitudes to trust Christ.

Among those who came forward was an old man with a long, white beard. He stood near the platform. For some reason, Billy Sunday was fascinated with that beard. He couldn't take his eyes from it. Finally, temptation overcame him and the unpredictable evangelist went to the edge of the platform, bent over, grasped the man's beard, and pulled it several times, saying "Honk, honk!"

*Can you imagine that?*

You and I might raise our eyebrows and say God couldn't use a man like that. Well, He did. Now God did not use him because of these foolish things. And I don't suggest that any would-be preacher go and do likewise.

But here is the point. Many a well-trained minister with all of the ecclesiastical accouterments (Dr. Tinkling Cymbal or Dr. Sounding Brass, for example) who trusts in his worldly knowledge and ability, has been passed by, and God in His wisdom has chosen instead to use a Billy Sunday to bring glory to Himself. And God did use Billy Sunday! Literally hundreds of thousands came to Christ through his ministry.

When I consider God using the "weak" things, I remember an episode that took place in a church I once pastored. We were having what we called a Week of Champions to reach the young people in that area for Christ. We invited many great athletes—professional and nonprofessional—to come and share their testimonies for Christ. The affair took place at the high school gymnasium. Among those who came was Paul Anderson, who at that time was reputed to be the strongest man in the world. What a specimen he was. He had biceps like coconuts.

He was asked, "Were you ever a ninety-seven-pound weakling?"

He said, "Yes, when I was four years old!"

His testimony was clear and strong. He said, in effect, "If the strongest man in the world needs Jesus, so do you."

The next Sunday, a young man came forward in our church service to confess Christ publicly as Lord and Savior. After visiting with him, I found he was converted the night Paul Anderson was present.

"What was it that Mr. Anderson said that touched your heart?" I asked.

"Oh, it wasn't what Paul said; it was what George Wilson said that reached me."

George Wilson? I couldn't remember which athlete he was. Then I recalled George was a paraplegic in a wheelchair who gave his testimony during a time of open sharing afterwards. He wasn't even a part of the official program. But he spoke of the joy of the Lord with a face shining like the noonday sun. That young student said to me, "When I saw the happy expression on the face of George Wilson, I thought that if God could do that for a man in a wheelchair, perhaps He could do something for me."

I have never forgotten that episode. On a night when the strongest man in the world was present, God used a crippled man in a wheelchair to bring a college student to Christ.

And what about the "base" things? Do you remember the story of Gideon? He was about as ignoble and base as a man could be. He lived in a time of great trouble in Israel. The enemy Midianites had overrun the land with their fierce warriors. Gideon was threshing wheat when the angel of the Lord appeared and said to him, ". . . the Lord is with thee, thou mighty man of valor. . . . Thou shalt save Israel from the hand of the Midianites . . ." (Judg. 6:12,14).

Gideon must have looked over his shoulder to see to whom the angel was speaking. And when it dawned on Gideon that *he* was being called the mighty man of valor, he quickly protested, "O my Lord, wherewith shall I save Israel? . . . behold, my family is poor in Manasseh, and I am the least in my father's house" (Judg. 6:15).

What Gideon was saying was something like this: "Of all the tribes in Israel, Manasseh is the worst; and of the families in Manasseh, my family is the poorest; and of all of the kids in my family, I am the runt of the litter." But this is just who God wanted—a man base enough that God could display His glory through him. And if you remember the story, you know that God made Gideon reduce the size of his army to only three hundred soldiers. It was then that He took a nobody general and a nothing army, defeated the Midianites and got the glory. God has chosen the base things of this world for His use.

Here is one more illustration of this exciting principle. When I think of "despised" things that God has chosen, I think of young David who later became the king over all Israel. The episode I have in mind is David's historic battle with Goliath of Gath.

There in the valley of Leah, about fifteen miles due west of Bethlehem, is the scene of the confrontation. The armies of Israel and the forces of the Philistines were joined in battle for almost six weeks. Goliath, a monstrous giant almost ten feet tall and covered with brass armor, stepped forward and delivered his challenge to fight single-handedly with a Hebrew. He would raise his ham-like fists to heaven and blaspheme the God of Israel and ridicule and taunt the children of God. Who would want to take that challenge? Even mighty Saul was quaking in his boots.

David was there that day. He was just a lad, a teen-age boy with a little peach fuzz on his chin. But there was something in David that was stirred to white-hot indignation when he heard the name of the thrice-holy God of Israel being mocked.

In the face of derision and certain scorn, David went forth to meet Goliath. He was armed with but a sling and five smooth stones.

There was a fundamental difference in David and everyone else that day. All the others were mumbling, "Look how much bigger Goliath is than we are." But David was thinking, "Look how much smaller than God Goliath is." The others were saying, "He's too big to hit." David was thinking, "He's too big to miss!"

At this point let's join the scriptural account. It thrills me every time I read it.

And the Philistine came on and drew near unto David; and the man that bare the shield went before him. And when the Philistine looked about, and saw David, he disdained him: for he was but a youth, and ruddy, and of a fair countenance. And the Philistine said unto David, Am I a dog, that thou comest to me with staves? . . . And the Philistine cursed David by his gods. And the Philistine said to David, Come to me, and I will give thy flesh unto the fowls of the air, and to the beasts of the field. Then said David to the Philistine, Thou comest to me with a sword, and with a spear, and with a shield: but I come to thee in the name of the Lord of hosts, the God of the armies of Israel, whom thou hast defied. This day will the Lord deliver thee into mine hand; and I will smite thee, and take thine head from thee; and I will give the carcases of the host of the Philistines this day unto the fowls of the air, and to the wild beasts of the earth; that all the earth may know that there is a God in Israel (1 Sam. 17:41–46).

Goliath was saying, "When I get my hands on you, I'm going to break you into pieces and feed you to the pigeons." But David was not intimidated. He knew that the battle was the Lord's.

The key verse to me is the last part of the above passage where David declared the victory would be his and then gave us the reason—"that all the earth may know that there is a God in Israel." Don't miss that point.

For what would it have meant that day if the Philistines had put forth a giant and Israel also had a giant, and the Israeli giant defeated the Philistine giant? Not a thing in the world!

It would just have been a good fight—that's all.

But when a despised, unheralded teen-age boy, with his faith in God, wins such a victory, everyone is forced to confess that there is a God in Israel. Do you see why God enjoys using despised things, that He might get the glory?

## Because He Lives in Me

In the light of all this, let us, as temples of the living God, make a threefold application to our lives:

1. First of all, there is a rebuke to our pride. "That no flesh shall glory in his presence" (1 Cor. 1:29). God will not share His glory with another. How God hates the sin of spiritual pride. I have observed that God will keep using a person as long as that individual keeps giving God the glory.

Don't ever be like the woodpecker who, while pecking away on a pine tree, was stunned by a bolt of lightning that struck the tree and split it from top to bottom. Hardly able to believe his eyes, he backed off and looked at the damage for a few moments. Then he flew away and came back leading nine other woodpeckers. And with a great deal of swagger he said, "There it is, gentlemen, right over there!"

When we start to take the credit for what God does, then He stops doing it.

2. There is a reckoning of our power. "But of him are ye in Christ Jesus, who of God is made unto us wisdom, and righteousness, and sanctification, and redemption" (1 Cor. 1:30).

Don't ever insult God by saying He cannot use you. That is not humility—it is blasphemy! Christ is alive and well and lives in you if you have been saved. You are His temple. Don't say, therefore, "Lord, help me to use my love, my strength, my wisdom." Remember that God gives extraordinary power to ordinary people.

3. There is a response to our praise. "That, according as it is written, He that glorieth, let him glory in the Lord" (1 Cor. 1:31). Oh, how we ought to praise Him. What a

wonderful plan it all is. The great God who is big enough to make the mighty universe is small enough to live within my heart. I am a temple of God. He literally dwells in me. Hallelujah!

Why should we be so inhibited when we are so inhabited?

# Like a River Glorious

*Afterward he brought me again unto the door of the house; and, behold, waters issued out from under the threshold of the house eastward: for the forefront of the house stood toward the east, and the waters came down from under, from the right side of the house, at the south side of the altar. Then brought he me out of the way of the gate northward, and led me about the way without unto the outer gate by the way that looketh eastward; and, behold, there ran out waters on the right side.*

*And when the man that had the line in his hand went forth eastward, he measured a thousand cubits, and he brought me through the waters; the waters were to the ankles. Again he measured a thousand, and brought me through the waters; the waters were to the knees. Again he measured a thousand, and brought me through; the waters were to the loins. Afterward he measured a thousand; and it was a river that I could not pass over: for the waters were risen, waters to swim in, a river that could not be passed over (Ezek. 47:1–5).*

Ezekiel had a vision of a river that was flowing out from the temple of God. Since this book deals with temple truth, let's examine it to see how this vision can help us as we live to serve the Lord.

To say the least, the writings of Ezekiel are difficult to

understand. But of this I am certain: Every temple designed by God in the Old Testament is in some way a preview and an illustration of the Christian believer whose body is a temple of the Holy Spirit.

Therefore, apart from whatever else is pictured here by the prophet, I see a picture of the Christian with a river of revival flowing out of his life. With that in mind, let us examine the . . .

## Mysterious Source of the River

Ezekiel sees a river flowing out of the house—that is, the temple of God. Right away our minds should go to a startling event that took place in the ministry of Jesus which may explain what Ezekiel was speaking about. The Feast of Tabernacles was coming to a climax. This feast was the zenith of Israel's holy days. It was a time of joyous thanksgiving at the end of the harvest season.

The high point of this ceremony was when the priests would bring a golden flask from the fountain of Siloam and pour the contents into a basin near the altar. Jewish tradition says, "He who has not seen the rejoicing at the place of the water drawing has never seen rejoicing in his life" (The *Talmud*, Sukkah 5:1).

Imagine yourself there on that day at the height of the ceremony. The city is filled with rapturous shouts as the white-robed priest pours out the sparkling water. It was at that moment that Jesus cried out with a loud voice.

If any man thirst, let him come unto me, and drink. He that believeth on me, as the scripture hath said, out of his belly shall flow rivers of living water. (But this spake he of the Spirit, which they that believe on him should receive: for the Holy Ghost was not yet given; because that Jesus was not yet glorified.) (John 7:37–39).

Jesus could no longer be silent. He saw the hilarity, the joy, the shouting. He heard the sounding trumpets, but He knew how hollow it all was. His soul was stirred because He knew it was all a passing moment of religious fervor and excitement. Before long they would go back to their same old fears, habits, and lethargy. The passing excitement would soon evaporate, just as the pitiful amount of water in that golden pitcher would soon be less than a vapor.

And there He was! Jesus Christ was unveiling the water of life right in the midst of the ceremony. But they did not recognize Him. It was not ceremony but Christ, not ritual but reality that they hungered for. It will be a great day in any land when people stop enduring religion and start enjoying salvation!

So Jesus, with a heart full of compassion and urgency, cried, "If any man thirst, let him come unto me, and drink" and "out of his belly shall flow rivers of living water." Jesus made it clear that this river of which He spoke was the Holy Spirit.

Every Christian, therefore, is to have a river of refreshment and blessing flowing out of him as God's dear Holy Spirit expresses Himself through that Christian.

The ones to whom Jesus spoke—and still speaks—are the thirsty ones. Jesus prefaced His great promise with an "if." "If any man thirst" is the prerequisite. How thirsty are you? Those who are filled with the stagnant waters of carnality and self-love are seldom thirsty for the things of God. Even those Christians who know that they are empty may not be genuinely thirsty. My gasoline tank has often been empty, but never once has it been thirsty.

But thank God for some who may read these lines who have a burning and blistering thirst and are willing to pay any price so that thirst might be satisfied. A little girl asked her mother for a drink of water three times in one night.

Finally, in an exasperated tone, the mother said, "If you ask for water one more time, I am going to spank you." A while later the little girl said, "Mama, when you get up to spank me, will you please bring me a drink of water."

I believe that one reason we are unwilling to let go of the cheap toys of this world and drink of Jesus' fullness is that we have never really been that thirsty. Let a man have a burning, blistering thirst, and he will pay almost any price for water.

And how wonderful that we can have an everlasting supply. Jesus told the Samaritan woman of water that would *forever* quench her thirst (see John 4:13). Christians are going from Bible conference to Bible conference to get their cups filled. That will no longer be necessary if there is a river flowing from within us.

Meanwhile back to Ezekiel. He seems to be foretelling the same thing that Jesus spoke of—a river of revival as God's floods of spiritual power flow from the cleansed temple of the believer in Christ.

Notice that the river has a *humble source.* It flows from "under a threshold" (Ezek. 47:1). This river has a lowly beginning. Genuine revivals start when God's people are on their faces before Him.

Next it has a *holy source.* It flows past the altar. There can be no revival that does not flow past the altar. The altar speaks of sacrifice and cleansing. When we meet God at the altar, the river begins to flow.

So often we are crying to God for revival as though we must persuade God to send it. It is not our duty to persuade Him to do so, but to permit Him to do so when we come to the precious blood of Jesus for cleansing. There is no way that we can bypass the altar and receive the blessing.

And it has a *heated source.* Ezekiel tells us that this river flows from the east door of the temple. That was the door facing the sunrise. Also, it flows from the south side of the altar. That is the sunny side. How our cold and frigid lives need to be warmed with God's love and power. Our coldness is one reason we are missing the blessings of God's revival power.

Bobbie Burns, the great Scottish poet, went into a church hoping to find some spiritual warmth for the depression and chill that had settled upon him. But the church service was more like a funeral dirge held in a mausoleum. He failed to find any comfort in the congregation's coldness, so he took a hymnal and scribbled these words in it:

> *As cold a wind as ever blew,*
> *As cold a church and in it but few.*
> *As cold a minister as ever spak.*
> *Ye'll all be hot ere I come back.*

## Marked Course of the River

This sparkling and bubbling trickle of water that comes from under the threshold grows as it flows cascading down the mountainside.

Then brought he me out of the way of the gate northward, and led me about the way without unto the outer gate by the way that looketh eastward; and, behold, there ran out waters on the right side. And when the man that had the line in his hand went forth eastward, he measured a thousand cubits, and he brought me through the waters; the waters were to the ankles. Again he measured a thousand, and brought me through the waters; the waters were to the knees. Again he measured a thousand, and brought me through; the waters were to the loins. Afterward he measured a thousand; and it was a river that I could not pass over: for the waters were risen, waters to swim in, a river that could not be passed over (Ezek. 47:2–5).

The water is now surging in an ever-deepening and widening course. It is a supernatural river because it grows without any tributaries. Who can add anything to the all-sufficiency of God's Spirit?

Note the water is measured in five-hundred-yard increments. It is seen to go from ankle-deep to knee-deep, from knee-deep to waist-deep, and finally from waist-deep to water that was over their heads—water to swim in.

Here is a *deepening work of God*. The ankle-deep water may speak of walking in the Spirit. The knee-deep water may speak of praying in the Spirit. Water to the loins may speak of being strong in the Spirit. Then water to swim in may speak of the mighty reviving force of God that picks us up and sweeps us along in its fullness as it overwhelms us completely. What a glorious thought!

Now God asked Ezekiel a question. "And he said unto me, Son of man, hast thou seen this? . . . Then he brought me, and caused me to return to the brink of the river" (Ezek. 47:6). I want to see it, don't you? How I long for a deeper work of the Spirit of God in my own life. Oh God, how I long for that mighty river to flow from my life into my world.

But so many are not seeing the deeper work of God. We are so satisfied with the status quo. Dr. Vance Havner has well said, "We have sacrificed depth for width. So rather than having a mighty power dam, we have a stagnant swamp."

And where does the river flow? *It flows into the depressed places.* "Then said he unto me, These waters issue out toward the east country, and go down into the desert, and go into the sea: which being brought forth into the sea, the waters shall be healed" (Ezek. 47:8).

These waters flow from the temple mount downward. "These waters . . . go down." Those who have traveled in Israel know that the area that Ezekiel speaks of where the waters actually are headed is thirteen hundred feet below sea level—the lowest spot on the face of the earth. But just as gravity causes water to seek the deep places, grace causes the Spirit to seek the depressed places in men's hearts.

And what depression there is in this world around us. It affects the up-and-outs as well as the down-and-outs. College students entered a contest to write a definition of life for the college newspaper. Here are some entries that won honorable mention. "Life is a joke that isn't even funny." "Life is a jail sentence that we get for the crime of being born." "Life is a disease for which the only cure is death."

These are not the deprived and the underprivileged. These are young people who seem to have everything—but Jesus.

The glorious river of revival needs to flow into depressed lives like these. This river needs to touch the college student without Christ, the businessman with his problems, the homemaker and housewife who is reduced to tears because of the depressing situation in which she may find herself. Oh, that that river of love and power might flow from temples like you and me into the depressed places.

*It flows into desert places.* "These waters . . . go down into the desert." Ezekiel speaks of the Arabah or the Judean desert. Those who have seen it know how parched and barren it is. This desert speaks of the dry and fruitless lives that need the bubbling waters of revival.

The barrenness is not only in the lives of the unsaved, but in the lives of those who name the name of Jesus. The curse of twentieth-century Christianity is the desert of dry mediocrity in which so many Christians are living. Jesus has chosen and ordained us to a life of fruitfulness and fullness. Yet the average Christian is living a life of dry devotions, fruitless faith, and barren evangelism. He needs the refreshing and reviving touch of the river of life that will cause his desert to blossom and bloom.

*It flows into the deadly places.* "These waters . . . go into the sea." The sea that Ezekiel speaks of is the Dead Sea. Because the Dead Sea receives but does not give, except by evaporation, it has an extreme concentration of salt. It is twenty-five percent more salty than ocean water, and the magnesium bromine prevents organic life. Its waters are leaden and poisonous. Hence it is called the Dead Sea. Those who dwell in deadly places, those under the curse of death and judgment because of their sinfulness and selfishness need the touch of the healing waters that flow from the hearts of God's people.

There is indeed something deadly working in America. Americans, like the Dead Sea, have often taken in of God's blessings, but we have not given. No wonder God is judging us.

So many people are asking, "Is God going to judge America?" I am convinced that God *is* judging America. As I see soaring inflation, runaway crime, racial hatred, economic confusion, moral perversion, scandal in high places, the loss of face nationally and internationally, I cannot help but feel that all of these are the judgment of God upon a sinful and selfish society.

Oh, how America and all of the world needs revival. Only God's mighty river will flow into the deadly places.

## Mighty Force of the River

What a mighty force a river is. The relentless power of a river can produce a wonder like the Grand Canyon. A river seems to be unstoppable. Throw rocks at it if you wish, but it keeps on flowing. Dam it up, but it just rises higher until it overflows its banks and spreads all over the land.

The only way to stop a river is to cut it off at its source. Since this river flows from the temple of God, that is the only place where it can be stopped. It would seem that the

Christian himself is the only one who can stop this mighty flow of power. God forbid that we should be guilty of restricting the waters of God's love and power that should flow from us.

And what a life-giving force this water is. Water is so very common, but so very priceless. One writer said, "Water is used to cool engines, produce electricity, regulate temperatures. To produce one loaf of bread takes three hundred gallons. Between cattle rancher, butcher, packager, and processor, four thousand gallons of water will be used to put a pound of beef in the supermarket. The building of one automobile requires ten thousand gallons. The human body is seventy percent water. We are constantly losing this precious liquid, and if it's not replaced quickly, we will die."[1]

Notice that *where the waters flow, the trees will grow*. "Now when I had returned, behold, at the bank of the river were very many trees on the one side and on the other" (Ezek. 47:7). There will be life rather than a sterile desert of death. A healthy saint is pictured in the Bible as a "tree planted by the rivers of water" (Ps. 1). Therefore, a Spirit-filled believer should be like a river whose life will strengthen fellow believers. We are not to be reservoirs of truth but rivers of blessings to those around about us.

And *where the waters flow, the fish will go*.

Then said he unto me, These waters issue out toward the east country, and go down into the desert, and go into the sea: which being brought forth into the sea, the waters shall be healed. And it shall come to pass, that every thing that liveth, which moveth, whithersoever the rivers shall come, shall live: and there shall be a very great multitude of fish, because these waters shall come thither; for they shall be healed; and every thing shall live whither the river cometh (Ezek. 47:8,9).

Obviously God has more in mind in this majestic passage than mere fish. Jesus spoke of "fishing for men" (Matt. 4:19). He, of course, was speaking of winning the lost; but as we look at the modern church, we seem to be catching very few fish.

One reason our nets are empty is that—with all of our plans, propaganda, and paraphernalia—we are fishing in stagnant seas and polluted pools. Oh, what a harvest of souls there will be when true revival comes and rivers of revival flow!

Think of the events that took place on the day of Pentecost in Jerusalem. Because Pentecost was such a great festival, the city was gorged with people. Perhaps a million or more Jews were present at that time. How would the early church reach them? There were just 120 common people. They had no printing presses, radio, or television. But they became the center of attention and the "multitude came together" (Acts 2:6). What an opportunity to preach the gospel.

Why did they come together? Because where the river flows, the fish will go. The river of God's Holy Spirit was flowing that day, and three thousand fish were caught in the gospel net.

*Where the waters flow, the fruit will show.*

And by the river upon the bank thereof, on this side and on that side, shall grow all trees for meat, whose leaf shall not fade, neither shall the fruit thereof be consumed; it shall bring forth new fruit according to his months, because their waters they issued out of the sanctuary: and the fruit thereof shall be for meat, and the leaf thereof for medicine (Ezek. 47:12).

What is this succulent fruit that hangs in clusters from the bending bows of these evergreen saints? Is it not the fruit of the Spirit?

Listen to Paul. "But the fruit of the Spirit is love, joy, peace, longsuffering, gentleness, goodness, faith" (Gal. 5:22). Oh, how the world is hungry for this fruit. In reality, Paul is describing the character of Jesus. Each of these characteristics is but a facet of the dear Savior. We don't produce that fruit; we merely bear it when God's river is flowing from the temple.

Finally, *where the waters flow, the health will glow.* ". . . its leaf shall be for medicine" (Ezek. 47:12). Today the body of Christ is suffering from sickness that is a dishonor to its head, the Lord Jesus Christ. But where the river of revival flows in full power, weak and anemic saints will vibrate with spiritual vitality and health. Oh, what a day that will be!

Sad indeed that there should be so many spiritually sick saints when our great God has provided such miracle medicine.

Dear Reader, be honest. Is the river of revival flowing from the temple of your body? If not, remember that Jesus said that when we come to Him and drink, that river of living water will begin to flow from our innermost being. But He said that we must be thirsty in order to come. Ask Him to increase your thirst for the things of God.

> *Like a river glorious, Is God's perfect peace,*
> *Over all victorious, In its bright increase;*
> *Perfect, yet it floweth, Fuller ev'ry day;*
> *Perfect, yet it groweth, Deeper all the way.*

> —Frances R. Havergal

# Keeping
# a Clean House

*This then is the message which we have heard of him, and declare unto you, that God is light, and in him is no darkness at all. If we say that we have fellowship with him, and walk in darkness, we lie, and do not the truth: But if we walk in the light, as he is in the light, we have fellowship one with another, and the blood of Jesus Christ his Son cleanseth us from all sin. If we say that we have no sin, we deceive ourselves, and the truth is not in us. If we confess our sins, he is faithful and just to forgive us our sins, and to cleanse us from all unrighteousness. If we say that we have not sinned, we make him a liar, and his word is not in us (1 John 1:5–10).*

One of the marks of a true Christian is that he feels dirty when he has sinned. David was a man after God's own heart. Yet he sinned grievously. In his prayer of repentance, he cried out, "Wash me throughly from mine iniquity, and cleanse me from my sin" (Ps. 51:2).

David, a king who lived a life of royalty, bathed in his marble tub, slept on silken sheets, wore his regal robes, felt dirty when he sinned. "Wash me, cleanse me," he prayed. He needed a spiritual house-cleaning because of his sin.

The man who does not know the Lord will not be deeply affected by the grime of guilt. Sin may be so much a part of his nature that he may not even be aware of its presence. A sow, for example, is yet to feel dirty. To wallow is her way.

"But it is happened unto them according to the true proverb, The dog is turned to his own vomit again; and the sow that was washed to her wallowing in the mire" (2 Pet. 2:22).

The difference in the saint and the sinner is not so much in whether or not they can sin. Any human being is capable of sinning. It is the basic attitude toward sin that makes the difference. The saint lapses into sin and loathes it. The sinner leaps into sin and loves it.

I know in my own personal life, I have been made to feel dirty because of sin in my life. I came to Jesus and just as He cleansed the temple in His days on earth, He cleansed and forgave me. He made the temple of my body sparkling clean and fresh. And the on-going efficacy of His shed and sprinkled blood is there to keep me clean.

The apostle John gives a marvelous lesson on spiritual housekeeping in his first epistle. It has been a personal guide to me. I want to share it with you.

## The Consequences of a Christian's Sin

That which we have seen and heard declare we unto you, that ye also may have fellowship with us: and truly our fellowship is with the Father, and with his Son Jesus Christ. And these things write we unto you, that your joy may be full (1 John 1:3,4).

These verses speak of the joy of fellowship with the Father and His Son, the Lord Jesus Christ. This fellowship brings a joy that is full and complete. The great and costly consequence of sin in the life of a saint is the loss of this joy.

We do not lose our salvation when we sin, but if we persist we indeed will lose the joy of our salvation. Hear the prayer of the repenting David, "Restore unto me the *joy* of thy salvation" (Ps. 51:12, italics mine).

If you would like to know if you are backslidden and away

from God, you might take the joy test. It is very simple. Is there in your heart this very moment "joy unspeakable and full of glory" (1 Pet. 1:8)? If not, you are not in fellowship with the Father.

"Wait a minute!" you say. "No one can be happy all the time." I agree. But I did not speak of happiness. I spoke of joy. The two are not the same.

Happiness depends on what happens, and therefore we call it happiness. If your happenstances are good, then you are happy. If they are bad, you are unhappy.

Joy does not depend upon happenstance or circumstance. It comes from Jesus and He does not change. "These things have I spoken unto you, that my joy might *remain* in you, and that your joy might be full" (John 15:11, italics mine). Therefore, a promise of constant joy awaits us.

Happiness is like a thermometer. It registers conditions. Joy is like a thermostat. It regulates conditions. Paul said, "Great is my boldness of speech toward you, great is my glorying of you. I am filled with comfort, I am exceeding joyful in all our tribulation" (2 Cor. 7:4). Jesus also spoke of His joy when He was facing the cross.

There is only one thing that can steal away your joy—sin! And only one kind of sin—yours! It is not what others do to you that takes away your joy. It is your reaction to what they do that takes away that joy. Your wife, children, or boss cannot diminish your joy. They may grieve you or give you sorrow, but they cannot lay hands upon your joy. Only your reaction to what they do to you can take away your joy.

By the way, it is our reactions, not our actions, that show what we really are. I can more or less plan and control my life. But if you really want to know what I am like, watch me when someone insults me or steals my parking place. If you want to know what is inside a man, wait until someone jostles him and see what spills out.

The loss of joy in a saint is a terrible loss. The most miserable man on earth is not an unsaved man, but rather a saved man who is out of fellowship with the Lord. God, when He saves us, does not fix us where we cannot sin anymore. If He did, we would be robots. But He does fix us where we cannot sin and enjoy it.

## The Consequences of Concealing Sin

If we say that we have fellowship with him, and walk in darkness, we lie, and do not the truth (1 John 1:6).

If we say that we have no sin, we deceive ourselves, and the truth is not in us (1 John 1:8).

If we say that we have not sinned, we make him a liar, and his word is not in us (1 John 1:10).

To err is human—and to try to conceal it is, too! Notice in the above verses the repeated phrase, "If we say." It points out the deceitfulness of sin. Each of these statements is the revelation of the human heart's desire to conceal rather than to confess sin.

One act of deceitfulness builds upon another. The longer sin goes without confession, the worse it gets in its concealment and deception.

1. *Lying to others.* "If we say we have fellowship with Him and walk in darkness, we lie." The Christian who is beginning to grow cold is tempted to put up a front. He pretends he is in the fellowship. He wants others to think he is as spiritual as he has always been.

Moses had an encounter with God on the mountaintop. And as a result, his face shone so brightly that he wore a veil to hide the glory of God that was reflected from his countenance. Later, however, when that glory had faded, Moses still wore the veil. He now wore it not to hide the glory, but to hide the fact that the glory was no longer there. Many Christians in our churches are wearing a veil because the glory they once had from God has faded.

2. *Lying to self.* "If we say we have no sin, we deceive ourselves." Sin that is not quickly confessed is easily rationalized. "Maybe it is not sin after all." We can call it by another name—a mistake, an error in judgment, a glandular malfunction, or environmental reaction. The sad thing is that when we believe our own lies about our sin, we are doubly deceived. "If therefore the light that is in thee be darkness, how great is that darkness" (Matt. 6:23).

3. *Lying to God.* "If we say we have not sinned, we make him a liar, and his word is not in us." If the Spirit of God says we have sinned and we deny it, we are then lying to Him. And our lies to Him are a way of calling Him a liar. But for the grace of God, there would be no hope for a person who has gone this far in concealing his sin.

Oh, how we need to learn to confess sin early. There is a deadly deception and an inevitable spread of sin when it is not confessed.

## Conviction of Sin

"This then is the message which we have heard of him, and declare unto you, that God is light, and in him is no darkness at all" (1 John 1:5).

Thank God that He is light. Because of this, He turns the searchlight of His unspotted holiness onto every area of our lives. It is His light that reveals the dirt in His temple.

The wise Christian will open the doors and windows of the temple and let the Father flood His world with light. Never be afraid of the light. More foolish than a child afraid of the darkness is a Christian afraid of the light. It is time for all of God's children to come out of the twilight zone and into the Sonlight.

There is a vast difference between Holy Spirit conviction and a satanic accusation. The nature of Satan is to accuse. The Holy Spirit does not accuse the saints. He convicts them. Many Christians are living lives of subsurface misery because they do not know the difference between the two. Just how does the Holy Spirit convict the child of God of his sin?

1. *Legitimately.* The Holy Spirit will only convict you for unconfessed and uncleansed sin. Those sins that have been placed under the blood and have been forgiven have also been forgotten. God said, "I will remember their sins no more" (Jer. 31:34). Therefore, He never brings them up again.

The devil, however, loves to dredge up forgiven sin and accuse us with it over and over. He repeats the saga of your past for you just as long as you're willing to listen to the replays.

One man was counseling with his pastor. He was being tormented by the ghost of guilt. Some sin in his former days was haunting him. The pastor said, "Have you confessed it to God?" "O yes," he said, "I've confessed it a thousand times." The wise pastor said, "That is nine hundred and ninety-nine times too many. You should have confessed it once and thanked God nine hundred and ninety-nine times for forgiving you."

2. *Specifically.* If Satan cannot accuse us of cleansed sin, he will accuse us of imagined sin. Therefore, some Christians are going around feeling bad in no particular spot but mostly all over. They are not certain what they have done wrong, but they feel like they surely must have done something.

The Holy Spirit, however, is like a doctor making an

examination. If there is a sin in our lives, He will put His finger on the sore spot and press hard. There will be no doubt as to where the problem is. He will speak to us and say something like this, "You lied to your wife" or "You were harsh to your son" or "You are filled with envy."

There will be no need for morbid introspection. We do not need to be taking ourselves apart a little piece at a time looking for sin. Just open your heart up to the Light. The Holy Spirit will do His work. If He does not convict you of some sin by name, then it is probably the devil accusing you.

3. *Redemptively.* Satan accuses you to condemn you. The Holy Spirit convicts you in order that you might be cleansed. Accusation leads to despair. Conviction leads to confession, cleansing, and victory.

## Confession of Sin

"If we confess our sins, he is faithful and just to forgive us our sins, and to cleanse us from all unrighteousness" (1 John 1:9).

After true conviction, there must be true confession. The word "confess" literally means "to agree with" or "to say the same thing." Therefore, a genuine confession of sin is not simply an admission of that sin. Nor is confession realizing you got caught. Along with admission of wrong, there must be an agreement with God concerning the seriousness of the sin and that the blood of Jesus Christ cleanses you from it.

We must say about our sin what God says about it. We must take sides with God. When we have done that, we have truly confessed it.

The word "confess" is in the present tense which means that this is to be the habitual practice of the saint. A Spirit-filled Christian is quick to confess sin when he becomes aware of it. It becomes a way of life. There is instantaneous and continual confession.

Not only will we confess *continually*, but we should confess *completely*. Notice that our verse mentions "our sins" and not "our sin." Don't try to simplify your confession. Don't kneel and say, "I confess all my sins." When the Holy Spirit convicts you specifically, then you should confess specifically.

Sometimes I get a pen and paper and write down those areas where the Spirit of God has convicted me. I have to tell you it really *hurts* to write these sins down and look at them. But it has been a very good experience for me.

We sing a little song:

"Count your many blessings, Name them one by one.
And it will surprise you what the Lord hath done."

Perhaps also, we could say,

"List your many failures, state them one by one.
And it will surprise you just what you have done."

But never stop there! After I have made my list, I confess my sins one by one. I claim victory and absolute cleansing by the blood of Christ and tear up the list. I am careful that no one else will ever find it, and I know God forgives and forgets.

I am convinced that many of God's children never have the joy of full forgiveness because they sin retail and confess wholesale. Deal with sin *completely*.

Finally, confess *confidently*. Remember that our loving heavenly Father is "faithful and just to forgive us our sins, and to cleanse us from all unrighteousness" (1 John 1:9).

Every sin that you have ever committed was totally paid for at Calvary—even those you did willfully and those which have caused permanent damage. Do you find that difficult to receive? Listen, by the grace of God, Jesus Christ paid for "the sins of the whole world" (1 John 2:2). Certainly that covers your sins, including the very worst of them.

If God did not forgive and cleanse *everything* we confess, He would be a liar (unfaithful) and a crook (unjust). But our God is faithful and just. It is not a matter of my feeling, but a matter of His faithfulness.

And pay close attention to that big little word "all." He says "all unrighteousness." And again, "The blood of Jesus Christ his Son cleanseth us from *all* sin" (1 John 1:7, italics mine). There are no sins that He will not cleanse.

Hallelujah! Every stain, every spot, every blur, every blot, every blemish in your life may be washed whiter than snow. And what God calls clean, let no man call unclean. Even you do not have the right to hold back God's forgiveness of you.

One more word. It makes no difference how many times you have failed; He will still forgive. Many times we fail over and over in the same area of our lives. We are ashamed to come and ask God for forgiveness. "Surely His patience must be worn out," we think. "He keeps forgiving and I keep failing."

Now what I am about to say is not to minimize sin. If you are continually failing in an area, perhaps you need to seek counsel from your pastor to become more consistent in Christ and victorious. But that is not the point here. I want to tell you with all of the emphasis of my soul that *if you have honestly confessed, He will forgive you no matter how many times He has forgiven you in that same area before.*

After all, it may seem like many other times to you; but from God's marvelous point of view, it is really like the first time you ever came to Him with that sin. Why? He forgot all the other times. For He remembers our iniquities against us no more.

I recently learned of a little girl who had been put in bed

for her afternoon nap. Mother was in the kitchen, cleaning up the dishes from lunch. In between scrubbing the plates, noises from the bedroom indicated the child was jumping up and down on the mattress, not sleeping.

"Settle down," the mother told her daughter as she peeked into the room through a slightly opened door. "You need your sleep, and besides before you know it, you'll break the lamp on the bedside table." It was a beautiful lamp, a prized possession in the family.

Minutes later, the jumping resumed. Then came the predictable crash. "I'm really sorry," the little girl sobbed after her spanking as mother cleaned up the broken glass.

When the mess was removed to the trash can, the mother came back to the room, hugged the child and said, "I forgive you. And as far as the lamp is concerned, I'll never mention it to you again."

The very next day the mother was walking through the house and inadvertantly stepped on and crushed the daughter's favorite doll. The little girl ran over and picked up the broken form, held it close and said, "Mommy, I forgive you, and I'll never mention it to you again."

Forgiveness is contagious. God not only cleanses you, He promises not to bring it up again. Ever. And when this assurance of sins forgiven becomes yours, you can forgive yourself—and others, too—and not ever mention it again.

The message of the written word is clear: "If we confess our sins, he is faithful and just to forgive us our sins, and to cleanse us from all unrighteousness" (1 John 1:9). Confess your sins. Then drop them. Forget them. God has.

Now move out in faith in the confidence that you are clean.

# Keeping Your Doors Locked

*For though we walk in the flesh, we do not war after the flesh: (For the weapons of our warfare are not carnal, but mighty through God to the pulling down of strongholds;) Casting down imaginations, and every high thing that exalteth itself against the knowledge of God, and bringing into captivity every thought to the obedience of Christ (2 Cor. 10:3–5).*

Your mind is a valued trophy over which a fierce battle is constantly being waged. Paul likens the human mind to a citadel or a stronghold that is the focal point of a strategic war. In this chapter we want to concern ourselves with toughening God's temple, specifically our minds, that we might operate effectively in spiritual conflict.

Notice that in the above passage Paul is speaking of warfare concerning the thought life. In these verses he mentions "imaginations," "knowledge," and "thought." No doubt about it, the human mind is the battlefield in spiritual matters. Mighty forces are striving for the citadel of your mind!

God wants your mind because He wants you. You are His temple. You have been bought with a price. It is quite obvious that if He does not control your thoughts, He will not control His temple. The command to every Christian is to "love the Lord thy God . . . with all thy mind" (Matt. 22:37).

But why is the human mind so crucially important? Simply because *we are what we think.* ( I sometimes think it's a wonder I didn't turn into a girl back in high school!) "For as he thinketh in his heart, so is he" (Prov. 23:7). This verse tells us the thought is the father of the deed. An old proverb puts it this way: "Sow a thought and you reap a deed. Sow a deed and you reap a habit. Sow a habit and you reap a character. Sow a character and you reap a destiny."

The whole process starts in the area of thought, in the mind itself.

## Satan's Desire

It goes without saying that Satan wants your mind. "But I fear, lest by any means, as the serpent beguiled Eve through his subtilty, so your minds should be corrupted from the simplicity that is in Christ" (2 Cor. 11:3). What a horrible concept—a corrupted mind! Satan wants to capture, control, and corrupt the thought life of the sons of men.

Further, the devil knows he can disgrace the testimony of a sincere Christian and bring heartache and ruin if he can first capture his control center, the mind. If Satan can get us to think a wrong thing, it is likely he will push us to do a wrong thing.

The enemy is aware that God has already destroyed the entire civilization of Noah's day because of evil imaginations.

> And God saw that the wickedness of man was great in the earth, and that every imagination of the thoughts of his heart was only evil continually. And it repented the Lord that he had made man on the earth, and it grieved him at his heart. And the Lord said, I will destroy man whom I have created from the face of the earth; both man, and beast, and the creeping thing, and the fowls of the air; for it repenteth me that I have made them (Gen. 6:5–7).

Indeed Satan knows the awesome but destructive power of a corrupted mind.

## Satan's Devices

The devil has a well-laid plan—a strategy, if you will—to work havoc in the thought life. We need not guess what it is for Paul has said, "We are not ignorant of his devices" (2 Cor. 2:11). Paul had pulled the veil of darkness from the enemy and exposed his methods.

*Satan blinds the mind of the unsaved.* Satan, the god of this age, has "blinded the minds of them which believe not, lest the light of the glorious gospel of Christ, who is the image of God, should shine unto them" (2 Cor. 4:4). A spiritually blinded mind is one that cannot see or perceive spiritual truth. His eyes need to be opened to Christ. This explains why Jesus said, "Except a man be born again, he cannot see" (John 3:3).

A young man, who was a gifted communicator, wrote the newspaper in a Florida city to tell the reading public why he was an atheist. It seemed he had dipped his pen in acid. He concluded his letter to the editor by saying, "When people finally stop praying to a non-existent God to save them from a non-existent hell, then maybe one more time the world will be populated by men rather than sheep."

Sometime later that young man was given the good news of Christ by a Spirit-filled Christian who had prayerfully asked God to open his blinded eyes. God in mercy broke through the midnight darkness of this young atheist's mind with a shaft of gospel sunlight. He was born again and could finally see.

I spoke to him shortly after his conversion. He wanted to become a baptized member of our church. He said, "Brother Rogers, it's so amazing what has happened to me. Before

God opened my heart, I was so sure that He did not even exist. But now all of that has changed and I can hardly remember the argument I used for my atheism."

Don't scold a blind man for not seeing. He cannot see. Pray for him. Bind the powers of darkness and loose the powers of Light by your prayers of intercession. "And I will give unto thee the keys of the kingdom of heaven: and whatsoever thou shalt bind on earth shall be bound in heaven: and whatsoever thou shalt loose on earth shall be loosed in heaven" (Matt. 16:19).

*Satan corrupts the minds of the saved.* Don't think that salvation means automatic immunity from satanic attack on your mental fortress. Paul had an apprehension concerning the saints at Corinth. "But I fear, lest by any means, as the serpent beguiled Eve through his subtility, so your minds should be corrupted from the simplicity that is in Christ" (2 Cor. 11:3).

And because Christians can have corrupted minds, there are saints across the world filled with anxieties and fears. Chilling inner doubts have come to hide the star of hope. Impurities—unclean pictures—are hung on the walls and corridors of the mind. Cares and worries wear away the health like sand wears away machinery. Deceptions and false doctrines neutralize and destroy the faith and testimony of the saints. Oh, the tragedy of corrupted minds!

## The Devil's Doors

You might ask, "How does the devil gain entrance into the Christian's thought life?" He comes in through unguarded doors. The Great Wall of China did not keep out the enemy. All that was necessary was to bribe a gatekeeper and the enemy was in. I want to mention three unguarded doors through which Satan enters the citadel of the soul to corrupt the minds of God's children.

1. *The perverse mind.* Unconfessed, harbored sin in any life is the devil's opened door.

> And be renewed in the spirit of your mind; and that ye put on the new man, which after God is created in righteousness and true holiness. Wherefore putting away lying, speak every man truth with his neighbor: for we are members one of another. Be ye angry, and sin not: let not the sun go down upon your wrath: Neither give place to the devil (Eph. 4:23–27).

Did you see it? "Neither give place to the devil." The thought expressed by Paul is this: When any Christian allows the sun to set on his sin, he has given the devil a place from which to work. That place is the unconfessed sin, which becomes a foul nest from which Satan can hatch his hellish ideas. That unconfessed sin becomes a stronghold from which Satan hurls his fiery darts of doubt. That unconfessed sin becomes Satan's legal ground from which he will not budge. By unconfessed sins the Christian can give him that place in which to camp.

Look again at the Scripture in Ephesians 4, and you will see that this sin may be an *attitude* (anger, bitterness, wrath, malice) as well as an *act.* Have you given the enemy a beachhead, a foothold, a campground? Unconfessed sin is a very dangerous matter for the child of God.

2. *The passive mind.* Another door many Christians have opened to Satan is a mind that is not aggressively controlled and kept by the believer. Our minds are to be actively guarded and never wandering or passively neglected. Solomon wisely warned, "Keep thy heart with all diligence, for out of it are the issues of life" (Prov. 4:23).

What does it mean to "keep your mind?" It means to guard it, control it, and never release it to anyone or anybody other than to the Lord. If you become passive and fail to think for yourself, a foreign power will take up the slack. Thoughts can be planted in your heart and mind. Judas was thinking Satan's thoughts after him when he betrayed Jesus. John makes this clear. "And supper being ended, the devil having now put into the heart of Judas Iscariot, Simon's son, to betray him" (John 13:2).

Of course Judas, the son of perdition, was void of spiritual life. But Satan has the power to put suggestions into the thoughts of God's children also. I'm amazed at the willingness with which people are throwing open the doors of their minds by passivity. Transcendental meditation (TM) still seems to be in vogue these days. The idea in TM is that if one can bring himself to a certain state of mental passivity, he will make contact with reality. He will make contact all right, but it just may be with the reality of the powers of darkness.

You wouldn't open all the windows and doors of your house and then go to sleep at night just to see what might come in, would you? Who in his right mind would welcome such unscrutinized guests? Christian friend, never turn your conscious mind over to anybody or anything. Keep it with all diligence. Spiritism, hypnotism, yoga, transcendental meditation, and suchlike are just unlocked doors and opened windows. Don't be so foolish.

Even amusement can lead to passivity. It is interesting to consider what "amuse" really means. "Muse" means to think, but when we add the prefix "a," it means not to think. When we are being amused, we are not really thinking. Our needs are in neutral and are by-passed.

Earl Radmacher has said,

> Human beings . . . don't exercise very much care about what they feed into God's computer, the brain. It's amazing how much 'garbage' some people will program into the brains as

they sit for hours in front of the T.V. It has been estimated that by the time a person in our society reaches the age of 18, he has watched 25,000 hours of television, including 350,000 commercials. (You know how intellectually stimulating commercials are!)

Am I overly concerned about the adverse effect of television on the human mind? I don't think so. Sometime ago, I was reading *Media and Methods,* the stock and trade magazine for communication people, when I came across a provocative statement by Herbert Marshall McLuhan, who is a giant in the field of communication. McLuhan affirmed, 'Only mad men would use television if they knew the consequences.'[1]

Many of the programs that are being watched by the American public are situation comedies (sitcoms) that make a mockery of sin. Harmless, you say? Look, the devil knows that once we have laughed at sin, it is difficult for us to think seriously about it anymore.

God has warned that His children should always have control of their minds, even when they worship Him. God does not work by putting the Christian into a blind trance or stupor. His method is not to step outside of your mind or to do an end-run on your intellect. He renews your mind and uses it. We may meditate as Christians, but our meditation will be centered on Christ. We are to gird up the loins of our minds. "Thou wilt keep him in perfect peace, whose mind is *stayed* on Thee" (Is. 26:3, italics mine).

3. *The polluted mind.* The use of drugs and intoxicants is the third unguarded door that lets Satan slip through to corrupt the thought life.

Sorcery is warned against clearly in the Scriptures. The word "sorcery" is a translation of the Greek word *pharmakeia.* It is the word from which we get our word "pharmacy." It means one who enchants with drugs. Drug abuse is a form of instant insanity that opens the doors to mind control by the enemy.

And I mean more than psychedelic drugs. Beverage alcohol is a dangerous drug. Dr. Jack Van Impe has called it, "the beloved enemy." He quotes Dr. Marvin Block, Chairman of the American Medical Association's Committee on Alcoholism, as saying: "Ours is a drug-oriented society, largely because of alcohol. Because of its social acceptance, alcohol is rarely thought of as a drug. But a drug it is, in scientific fact."[2]

Van Impe also quotes former Iowa Senator Harold Hughes as saying: "Many people think alcohol is a stimulant. Others call it a depressant, but it's a drug—dirty, vicious, and brutal. It's the mainstay drug of the American-built society."[3]

One man bragged that he drank vodka so no one could smell liquor on his breath and know he was drinking. His friend said, "If I were you, I would drink something else. It would be better for them to know you are drunk than to think you are stupid."

Not only is it stupid, it is sad.

Many Americans who claim to be Christians have opened the door to mind control by the devil through sorcery or the use of drugs. Beware of the polluted mind!

## Satan's Defeat

Thank God it is possible for His children to actively recapture the fortress of their minds. If you have misused your mind, I have good news and hope to offer. "For though we walk in the flesh, we do not war after the flesh: (For the weapons of our warfare are not carnal, but mighty through God to the pulling down of strongholds)" (2 Cor. 10:3,4).

Clearly, Paul says there is victory for the child of God. But carnal weapons are not sufficient for this spiritual battle. The battle for the mind will never be won by education, psychology, psychiatry, or positive thinking. These all have a proper place, but one might as well throw snowballs to stop a B-1 Bomber as to try to dislodge Satan's thought patterns with such carnal weapons.

I want to mention three mighty weapons that will secure and guard the mind of the believer who has suffered invasion by the enemy.

1. *For the perverse mind there is repentance.* Don't ever think that only the unsaved need to repent. Jesus' last word to the church was not the Great Commission. It was "repent." Five of the seven churches of Asia in the Book of Revelation are commanded by Christ to repent.

The Greek word for repentance is *metanoia.* It literally means "a change of mind." There is no way to deal with the perverse mind but to change it. The sin that has become Satan's foul nest and legal territory must be uprooted and removed.

Repentance always leads to confession, and confession leads to cleansing, and it is cleansing that takes away the place given to the devil, spoken of in Ephesians 4:27. How wonderful when the cleansing tides of Calvary wash over the soul, and the fresh breeze of the Spirit sweeps through the mind.

Why is it that we modern Christians are willing to try almost everything today but good old-fashioned repentance? Are there areas of stronghold in your mind right now over which you need to exercise some mind-changing repentance? Is God the Holy Spirit telling you that you need to repent? Turn from these things now, this moment! If you won't do this, I don't think there is much else I can say to you that will help. Come to Christ with a soft heart and repent of your sins.

2. *For the passive mind there is resistance.* James tells us how

to resist. "Submit yourselves therefore to God. Resist the devil, and he will flee from you" (James 4:7). Why should we resist? Because Satan will not give up anything or anybody without a struggle. And how can we resist? Do what you know is right. Say no to sin. Make certain that every sin is confessed. Make sure that you have taken back every place you yielded. And then ask the Lord to rebuke Satan (see Jude 9). Remember, he now has no legal right. He *must* flee.

You may want to say, "I resist the enemy in the name of Jesus. He has no right or authority in my life. My body is the temple of the Holy Spirit. I am bought with the price of the blood of Christ. He cannot trespass on my Father's property. May the Lord rebuke him!"

3. *For the polluted mind there is renewal.* Minds that have been damaged and distorted can be made over. New thought patterns can and must be established. Listen to these marvelous promises.

And be renewed in the spirit of your mind (Eph. 4:23).

I beseech you therefore, brethren, by the mercies of God, that ye present your bodies a living sacrifice, holy, acceptable unto God, which is your reasonable service. And be not conformed to this world: but be ye transformed by the renewing of your mind, that ye may prove what is that good, and acceptable, and perfect, will of God (Rom. 12:1,2).

God will renew your mind after you repent and resist. It will be done as you change the focus of your attention. Remember that we become what we think about.

Now here's the exciting part: God has so engineered your mind that you cannot think two thoughts at one time. So if you are thinking what is right, you can't be thinking what is wrong. Paul stated it so beautifully. "Finally, brethren, whatsoever things are true, whatsoever things are just, whatsoever things are pure, whatsoever things are lovely, what-soever things are of good report; if there be any virtue, and if there be any praise, think on these things" (Phil. 4:8).

Now let me give you this word of advice about the re-newed mind. Don't try not to think wrong thoughts. That never works. For example, for the next thirty seconds, what-ever you do, don't think about an elephant. If my guess is right, that's about all you can think about when you are trying not to think about an elephant. Right?

Here's the way to do it. Just get up each morning and bathe your soul in the presence of Jesus. Talk with Him, first off, in prayer. Then saturate your mind with His Word. "Let the word of Christ dwell in you richly in all wisdom; teach-ing and admonishing one another in psalms and hymns and spiritual songs, singing with grace in your hearts to the Lord" (Col. 3:16). Commit your day to Him. Before long, it will become evident that God is renewing your mind.

The doors of your temple can be shut to the enemy, and the windows of your soul can be open to the Lord.

# C H A P T E R   1 0

# A House
# of Prayer

*And he taught, saying unto them, Is it not written, My house shall be called of all nations the house of prayer? . . . but ye have made it a den of thieves (Mark 11:17).*

As temples of the Holy Spirit, our bodies should be houses of prayer. Anything that distracts from vital prayer in our lives is a treacherous thief. It steals from us the blessings the Father longs to bestow, and it takes from the Father the glory that He so richly deserves.

What fools we are to allow ourselves to be so robbed. We desperately need to learn the art of prevailing prayer. Prayer is so fantastic because it links us with the almighty God in a miraculous way. Prayer can do anything that God can do, and God can do anything.

One day, as I was meditating, one of the most electrifying thoughts I have ever had came into my heart. I cannot tell you the impact that it made on me. Yet this thought is so simple and presumably so well-known that I almost hesitate to tell you about it. Are you ready for it? Well, here it is. God hears and answers prayer! Oh, you say, every Christian knows that. Yes, so did I in my head. But somehow I saw the truth of that truth, and it shook me to my very foundations.

I thought, "If this is true, and it is true, then the one thing above everything that I should learn to do is to pray." There can be no greater achievement than a vital prayer life. I challenge you now to stop and really consider the impact of this thought with me—that we as mortals can link our nothingness with God's almightiness through prayer. I say it again—what fools we are if we do not learn to pray.

Failure to pray is a tragedy, but it is more than a tragedy. It is a sin. God says in 1 Samuel 12:23, "Moreover as for me, God forbid that I should sin against the Lord in ceasing to pray for you: but I will teach you the good and the right way."

With this in mind, I want to see what Jesus taught about prevailing prayer. Do not let your familiarity with the following passage keep you from giving it the full attention of your heart. What an amazing passage it is. The more we look at it, the more we see. It is sweet to the child, but perplexing to the scholar and beneficial for every one of us.

> After this manner therefore pray ye: Our Father which art in heaven, Hallowed be thy name. Thy kingdom come. Thy will be done in earth, as it is in heaven. Give us this day our daily bread. And forgive us our debts, as we forgive our debtors. And lead us not into temptation, but deliver us from evil: For thine is the kingdom, and the power, and the glory, for ever. Amen (Matt. 6:9–13)

Before Jesus gave this lesson on prayer, He had just warned against praying only to be seen by men. I heard of a young lawyer who had just opened up a brand new office. He was seated behind his shiny new desk eagerly awaiting his first client. Soon he heard footsteps in the hall and then a hand upon the doorknob. Wanting to look important he pretended to be busy, so he picked up the telephone and carried on a fake conversation. "Yes, yes, I'll have my secretary tend to that when I can get at it. I have a very heavy schedule before me. Call me back in a few days." He then motioned toward the door, "Come in, come in." The stranger was now in the office listening to one end of this high-level conversation. Finally the receiver was put back on the hook and the lawyer turned to what he hoped was a prospective client. "Now what may I do for you."

The man answered, "I'm from the phone company, and I came to connect your telephone."

So much of our praying is like that. We are praying to be seen by men, but no one is on the other end of the line. Wouldn't you like to quit playing games and get down to serious business in this matter of prayer? Let's allow the Lord Jesus, the Master Teacher, to show us how.

## The Person of the Prayer

*Our Father.* Notice how Christ's model prayer begins. Right away we learn that vital prayer is a child talking with his Father. Because this is so, several other truths come quickly to our hearts.

First, we must be children of God in order to pray with effectiveness. Not everyone has the right to call God "Father." Just those who have been born into His family have that right.

Do I hear someone protesting, "Wait a minute, God created everybody and so God is the Father of everybody." I beg to differ. He is not the Father of everybody. God does not become Father by creation. He created cats and dogs, flies and frogs, but He is not their Father. He is only their Creator.

God makes it clear in the Scriptures that some human beings are not children of God. Jesus said of the unconverted Pharisees, "Ye are of your father the devil" (John 8:44). We become children of God and can only call Him "Father" when by faith we receive Christ as our Lord and Savior and are born into His family. John makes this clear. He speaks concerning Jesus and says, "He came unto his own, and his own received him not. But as many as received him, to them gave he power to become the sons of God, even to them that believe on his name" (John 1:11,12).

But if He is your Father, how simple and natural it ought to be for you to pray. Some think that one has to use the language of a Shakespeare in order to pray. This is not so! Jesus said, "But when ye pray, use not vain repetitions, as the heathen do; for they think that they shall be heard for their much speaking" (Matt. 6:7).

Suppose my daughter meets me when I come home and says, "Oh, hail thou eminent pastor of Bellevue Baptist Church. I beseech thee that thou wouldest grant to thy daughter, whom thou lovest, some financial assistance that she may sojourn to yon apothecary for some cosmetical necessities."

I think I would say, "Huh?"

Wouldn't it be much better if she would simply say, "I love you, Daddy. I am so glad you are home. Say, I need five dollars to get some things at the drugstore."

Remember, God is your Father. The Holy Spirit has even taught us to pray, "Abba, Father" (Rom. 8:15). *Abba* is an Aramaic word that is very close to our word "Daddy." It was one of the first words framed upon the lips of a little baby. How thrilling to know that, as God's dear child, you can come with such intimate confidence as to call Him "Abba, Father." Is He truly your Father?

## The Purpose of the Prayer

*Thy will be done.* We are told to pray "Thy kingdom come, thy will be done." This tells us immediately that prayer has one very major purpose and that purpose is to seek and to secure the will of God. Prayer is answered only when it is in the will of God. "And this is the confidence that we have in him, that, if we ask any thing according to his will, he heareth us" (1 John 5:14). Someone has wisely said that "Nothing lies beyond the reach of prayer except that which lies outside the will of God."

Someone may ask, "Oh, do you mean that in my praying I am restricted to the will of God?" My dear friend, don't be concerned about that. For you to worry about being restricted by the will of God would be like a minnow being concerned about being hemmed in by the Atlantic Ocean.

Praying in the will of God does not mean fewer blessings for you, but greater blessings for you. God wants for you what you would want for yourself if you only had enough sense to want it. We should never fear the will of God.

But remember that prayer is not some exercise whereby we try to bend God's will to fit our wills. Prayer is not talking God into doing something that He ordinarily would not want to do. Prayer is the thrilling experience of finding God's will and then asking Him for it.

Now that brings into focus a very key point and question. Just how do we know God's will? Obviously God's will is made known in a general sense as we read the Bible, but there are so many specific things that the Scriptures do not touch upon. There is no Scripture that tells us what job to take, what girl to marry, (incidentally, proper prayer would help avoid many divorces—and quite a few marriages), or what school to attend.

The secret of knowing God's will in prayer is not only to know the Bible and let its truth abide in us, but to be very, very sensitive to the leading of the Holy Spirit of God. Remember that because you are a temple of God and a house of prayer, He, God's Holy Spirit, abides within you *and will help you pray.* The Bible calls this kind of praying "praying in the Spirit."

"Praying always with all prayer and supplication in the Spirit, and watching thereunto with all perseverance and supplication for all saints" (Eph. 6:18). "But ye, beloved, building up yourselves on your most holy faith, praying in the Holy Ghost" (Jude 20).

When we pray, we are to pray to the Father, through the Son, in the Spirit. What a glorious partnership there is between the Holy Spirit and the human spirit. He teaches us the will of God and helps us to pray as we ought. The Holy Spirit, as our helper, wants to think through our minds, feel through our hearts, speak through our lips, weep through our eyes, and express Himself through our spirits.

Perhaps one of the greatest truths I have ever learned about prayer is this: The prayer that gets to heaven is the prayer that starts in heaven. What we do is close the circuit.

I heard someone in the past give this definition of prayer: "Prayer is the Holy Spirit finding a desire in the heart of the Father and then placing that desire into our hearts. The desire is then sent back to heaven in the power of the cross."

This is why we must learn to wait before the Father in meditation and openness when we pray. So often we simply rush into the presence of God and say, "Listen, Lord, your servant speaks" rather than saying, "Speak, Lord, your servant is listening."

Are you listening? Are you honestly seeking to know and do the will of God? Man's ruin began in the Garden of Eden. When the spirit of the first Adam said, "Not thy will but mine be done." Man's rescue came in another garden when the last Adam said, "Not my will, but thine, be done" (Luke 22:42).

The Spirit of the Lord Jesus is the Spirit that should characterize our praying.

## The Provision of the Prayer

*Give us this day our daily bread.* Surely we may ask for our needs. While we cannot pray selfish prayers, we certainly may pray personal prayers for personal needs. Our Father is concerned with every need we have.

Remember that this model prayer we are studying is but a guide for praying. I do not believe that Jesus meant we should only ask for bread. What He did mean was that we should bring all of our needs to the Father and ask Him specifically for what we need.

Paul reminds us, "My God shall supply all your need according to his riches in glory by Christ Jesus" (Phil. 4:19). I am so very glad He didn't say "out of his riches." He said, "according to his riches." A millionnaire may give you one dollar out of his riches, but that is not necessarily according to his riches. Think of the vast riches of our Father, and realize that He is ready to meet our needs according to those riches.

Also, I am very glad He didn't say "all your wants." He said, "all your need." I have sometimes wanted things I didn't need. And I have sometimes needed things I didn't want. For example, my Dad would say sometimes, "Adrian, you need a spanking." He was quite right, but of course, I didn't want one.

I believe many Christians have needs that are unmet, simply because they do not pray. James reminds us, "Ye have not, because ye ask not" (James 4:2). When I was a student-pastor in Florida, I shepherded a small church in Indian River County. You may not know, but the best citrus fruit in all of Florida grows there. One day as I was returning to college after serving my church on the weekend, a deacon in that church gave me several bushels of delicious oranges.

I said, "Mr. Ingram, I cannot eat all of those oranges before they spoil."

He said, "Well take them back to college, Adrian, and give them away."

So I took the oranges to college, lugged them upstairs to our apartment, and put them in a closet.

One day shortly after that, I looked from our second story out into our backyard and saw a little fellow about seven years of age sneaking around in a suspicious manner. He was looking every way but up. (Does that remind you of anyone you know?) I realized after a while he was going to steal an orange from the lonely orange tree in our backyard. I decided I would let him because the one thing he did not know was that our orange tree was a sour-orange tree. In Florida these sour-orange trees are a very beautiful ornamental shrub. But the fruit is extremely bitter. As a matter of fact, it is not fit for man nor beast.

I watched as he plucked his prize. Even though I was working my way through school, I believe I would have given a dollar to see him take that first bite.

Now the irony of the whole matter is this. Had he only knocked on my door and asked, "Mister, may I have one of those oranges?" I would have said no. But then I would have loaded him down with more of the best oranges than he could carry.

When we get to heaven, I wonder if the heavenly Father will not bring us to some huge cosmic closet and say, "Look in there. Do you see all of those things? They are the blessings that I longed to give you, but you never asked. You were enjoying the bitter fruit of your own scheming and wisdom rather than asking me for what is best."

Oh, let us learn to ask the Father for the things we need. Remember, there is nothing big enough to concern us that is too small to concern Him. Ask Him for your needs.

## The Pardon of the Prayer

*Forgive us our debts.* Powerful prayer must come from a clean heart. Jesus taught us to pray for daily forgiveness just as we pray for daily bread. Since we have already talked at length about confession and repentance, let me just say a few things by way of review.

The reason many of our prayers are not answered is that we are not including confession and repentance with our petitions. The prayer from a dirty heart is a prayer not answered.

We like to quote the prayer promises in the Holy Scriptures, don't we? Well, let me give you a prayer promise that we are prone to forget. It is "If I regard iniquity in my heart, the Lord will not hear me" (Ps. 66:18). Is there any iniquity that you have made peace with? Is there any sin, habit, grudge that you have regard for? If so, for God to answer your prayer would really be an encouragement for you to continue in that sin.

James warns all of us when he says, "Draw nigh to God, and he will draw nigh to you. Cleanse your hands, ye sinners; and purify your hearts, ye double-minded" (James 4:8). We cannot pray effectively with dirty hands, defiled hearts, and double minds.

Monkeys are captured in the South Sea Islands in an unusual way. The natives fasten a coconut with a hole in it to a tree. Some rice is placed inside the coconut. A curious monkey will examine the coconut and see the rice inside. He then puts his paw through the hole and grabs a fistful of rice. Now with his hand doubled up, it is too big to withdraw. The poor monkey will plead and scream as his captor approaches, but he will not release the rice so that he can withdraw his hand.

One wise man prayed like this, "Oh, Lord, help me to cooperate with you so you won't have to operate on me." Why don't you do the same? So many of us, it seems, would rather hold to our sins than to enjoy the freedom of a prayer life that knows no limits. Are there sins that have made your temple a den of thieves rather than a house of prayer? If so, pray, "Forgive me my debts." Then let go of your fistful of rice so God can stop chastising you and start blessing you.

## The Protection of the Prayer

*Deliver us from evil.* This phrase, "Deliver us from evil," could be stated "Deliver us from the Evil One." Satan is so very real. He has already made plans to sabotage your life and to hurt your loved ones. He has already dug a pit for your feet to fall in this day.

Now remember, his real war is with God. But he cannot get at God directly. He knows, as evil persons have always known, that if you cannot harm someone, then the next most effective thing is to harm someone that someone loves. God loves you and, therefore, Satan has aimed all of the artillery of hell at you. You need protection.

Your protection is provided through prayer. The prayer for deliverance from evil and temptation is preventive medicine. Though how prone we are to forget it. I feel certain that the reason we keep asking for forgiveness for the same old sins is that we have not been claiming our protection from the enemy.

Yet aren't you weary of the same old confessions? The reason that we fall into this trap is that we remember to pray "Forgive us." But we fail to pray "Deliver us."

What happens is something like this. We wake up a little late. We hurry through our devotions—or have none at all. But it's a new day anyway and nothing has happened yet to upset us. Things are running smoothly. We catch a snatch of the newspaper and gulp down a little breakfast and dash off to work. (Why do they call it the rush hour when the traffic moves so slowly?) But we get our day started and everything seems to be going just fine. Then at an unsuspecting moment, Satan tosses a bombshell into our laps, and spiritually we are blown to smithereens. We fail miserably!

At the end of the day we try to clean up the mess. We bow before God and pray, "Forgive me my debts." And He does. But don't you see that the model prayer that Jesus has given is not a prayer for the end of the day. This is a morning prayer. Can you imagine someone coming to the end of the day and praying like this, "Lord, give me today my daily bread." And then off to sleep he goes. That would be foolish, wouldn't it? And just as in the morning we ask for provision, we are to ask for protection at the same time.

I have a professional football-player friend who likes to tell this story: "When I graduated from college, my coach said, 'Mike, would you help me do some scouting?' [For the uninitiated that means to look for some prospective football players to be enrolled in college.]

"I said, 'Sure, coach, what kind of player are you looking for?'

"He said, 'Well, there's the kind of guy that when you knock him down, he just stays down.'

" 'We don't want him, do we, coach?'

" 'No. Then there is the kind of guy that when you knock him down, he gets up. But if you knock him down the second time, he just stays down.'

" 'We don't want him either, do we, coach?'

" 'No, we don't. But there is the kind of guy that when you knock him down, he gets up; knock him down, and he gets up; knock him down, and he gets up; knock him down again, and he just keeps getting up.'

" 'That's the guy we want, right, coach?'

" 'No, we don't want him either. What I want you to do is find the guy who's knocking all the other guys down. That's the guy I want.' "

I say amen to that. I'm glad God enables us by His grace to keep getting up every time Satan knocks us down. But I think it is time that God's people got off the defensive and got on the offensive. It's time Satan started to flee from us. And he will when we begin the day by putting on the whole armor of God and bathing our souls in the presence and power of the Lord Jesus. Please don't forget the protection of the prayer.

## The Praise of the Prayer

*Thine is the glory.* Notice that Jesus' model prayer both opens and closes on a note of praise. And how appropriate this is. You see, prayer must be done in faith, and praise is the best expression of faith of anything I know. Praise is faith turned inside out.

When we ask God for things, that is petition. But petition without praise is unbelief. Praise without petition, however, is presumption. But when we link petition and praise together, that is power. When I ask God, then praise God, I am believing God. Petition says, "Please." Praise says, "Thank you."

If your faith is strong, your prayer will be strong. Pray and believe and you will receive. Pray and doubt and you will do without.

How important, therefore, it is that we learn to praise. I cannot overestimate the power of praise. If your prayer life seems useless and powerless, learn to praise God. The Bible says that God inhabits the praises of His people. He is so very near when we praise Him. Billy Sunday was right when he said that "we need to jerk some of the groans out of our prayers and shove in a few hallelujahs."

And why shouldn't we offer praise? Angel Martinez has noted that the Lord's Prayer begins "Our Father" and ends "Thine is the kingdom." He points out that our Father is a King.[1] Just think about that. Our Father is King. I have a Father who will hear me and a King who can answer me. I have the sympathy of a Father and the sovereignty of a King attuned to my prayer. Yes, why shouldn't I offer God praise?

You will discover victory when you let your temple be a house of prayer.

# A Heart
# Is Not a Hotel

*And I will pray the Father, and he shall give you another Comforter, that he may abide with you for ever (John 14:16).*

Is there a greater thought to bring comfort to the human heart than to know that we, sinful and weak as we are, may become temples of the living God? It is staggering to think of my body as His royal residence.

Yet there is perhaps an even more thrilling truth that Jesus has made known to us and it is this: When God moves into the human heart, He moves in to stay. Jesus said of the Holy Spirit that He will "abide with you forever."

The word "abide" may be translated "continue," "dwell," "endure," "remain," "stand." God has come to settle down in us. My friend Ron Dunn put it well when he said, "My heart is not a hotel with check-out time twelve noon on Sunday."

This abiding presence is what the theologians call the eternal security of the believer. It is a truth that ought to bring strength and joy to your heart.

Now when I speak of His abiding presence—the eternal security of the believer in Christ—I want to make something clear. I'm not speaking concerning the security of those who merely profess to be saved. There are many professors of salvation who are not possessors of salvation. Outwardly they may look, act, and talk like Christians, but they have never been redeemed.

Jesus spoke an emphatic word of warning concerning these pretenders who have never been born again. "Many will say to me in that day, Lord, Lord, have we not prophesied in thy name? . . . and in thy name have cast out devils? . . . And in thy name done many wonderful works? . . . And then will I profess unto them, I never knew you; depart from me, ye that work iniquity" (Matt. 7:22,23).

Note the phrase that Jesus used, "I never knew you." We have all seen some make a false start and then fall away and even deny the faith they once professed. They did not lose their salvation because they never had it. Jesus said, "I never knew you." I don't know who first coined this little statement, but it says it well: "The faith that fizzles before the finish had a flaw from the first."

I call these people, who start out fine and then fade away, "alka-seltzer Christians." You drop them in water, they fizzle a little bit, but then they disappear. John the apostle made reference to some of these alka-seltzer Christians when he said, "They went out from us, but they were not of us; for if they had been of us, they would no doubt have continued with us; but they went out, that they might be made manifest that they were not all of us" (1 John 2:19). Notice that they went out from us, because they were not of us. That is, they had never really been added to the body of Jesus through the new birth.

Think with me about seven wonderful reasons why someone who has been made a partaker of the divine nature can never ever again be a lost soul.

## The Perseverance of the Spirit

There is a wonderful truth expressed by the apostle Paul to the Philippians. "Being confident of this very thing, that he which hath begun a good work in you will perform it until the day of Jesus Christ" (Phil. 1:6). Who is it that has begun this good work in us, and who is going to carry it on to completion? The Holy Spirit, of course. And this verse says what He has begun He will finish.

Have you ever started anything you couldn't finish? I think this is a trait common to human nature. I heard of a youngster named Billy who said to his dad, "Daddy, Jimmy says that his dad has a list of men that he can whip, and your name is the first one on the list."

The next scene is Billy's daddy confronting Jimmy's daddy. "My son said that you have a list of men that you can whip, and my name is first on the list. Is that right?"

"Yes, that's right."

"Well, you can't do it! What are you going to do about that?" Billy's dad said.

"Then I guess I'll just have to take your name off the list," said Jimmy's dad.

It is not a trait of omnipotence, however, to start things that omnipotence cannot finish. When God saved us, our names were recorded in heaven, and God will never take our names off the list because He has not been able to finish what He began.

Just think what the Holy Spirit does in our salvation. He is the *Convicter*. He is the One who shows us our sins and brings us under conviction. He is also the *Converter*. He is the One who works the marvelous work of grace in our hearts so that we are "born of the Spirit" (John 3:8). And since He is the Convicter and the Converter, He is also the *Completer*. He will finish what He has begun. He will not abandon you as some half-completed relic.

## The Perfection of the Sacrifice

When Jesus died on the cross, He offered a perfect sacrifice that made us perfect forever. "For by one offering he hath perfected for ever them that are sanctified" (Heb. 10:14). In the Old Testament when a sacrifice for sin was made, it was never a perfect or a complete sacrifice. Those Old Testament priests had to come again and again with their bloody sacrifices to those smoking altars, because those sacrifices were only shadows and prophecies of that perfect sacrifice that would come.

> For the law having a shadow of good things to come, and not the very image of the things, can never with those sacrifices which they offered year by year continually make the comers thereunto perfect. For then would they not have ceased to be offered? because the worshipers once purged should have had no more conscience of sins. But in those sacrifices there is a remembrance again made of sins every year. For it is not possible that the blood of bulls and of goats should take away sins (Heb. 10:1–4).

All those sacrifices did were to roll the sins of the people forward one more year. But when Jesus shed His rich, red, royal blood on that cross, everything was paid in full. And because of that sacrifice, we are "perfected for ever." We don't get just a fresh start or a new chance, but an eternal perfection.

Think with me for just a moment. If it were possible for one to lose his salvation (which, of course, it isn't) then for that person to be saved the second time, Jesus would have to die the second time. What happened at Calvary was good for eternal salvation. It was "one offering" and it was "for ever."

It is for this reason that if you search the Scriptures through you will never find where anyone was ever saved twice. Our salvation is once for all, and if it is not "once saved, always saved," it would have to be "twice lost, always lost." Oh, how I thank God that when Jesus died for me, He perfected me forever.

## The Position of the Saved

When we are saved, not only does He come in to live in us, but we also take our position in Him. "Therefore if any man be in Christ, he is a new creature; old things are passed away; behold, all things are become new" (2 Cor. 5:17).

In this verse our position is clearly stated "in Christ." That means, among other things, that we are actually a part of His mystical body. For me ever to be separated from Him and be eternally lost would also mean that a part of Jesus was eternally lost. I have been made a part of His very body. Christ is the invisible part of the visible Christian. And a Christian is the visible part of the invisible Christ. We are in Him, and He is in us.

Peter tells us that our position in Christ is illustrated by Noah's position in the ark. (See 1 Pet. 3:18–22.) When that ark was finished, a perfect way of escape from the wrath of God had been provided.

The Old Testament tells us that the ark was covered "within and without with pitch" (Gen. 6:14). You should note that the Hebrew word for "pitch" is exactly the same word that is used elsewhere in the Bible for "atonement." Thank God for the atonement that keeps the waters of God's wrath from reaching His rescued ones.

Now Noah was not told to place pegs on the outside of the ark on which he might hold. This would have been ridiculous. Yet this is the kind of salvation some people think they have. They feel they can get to heaven if they can just hold out faithful to the end.

Imagine this scene. Noah is holding on to a slimy peg on the outside of the ark. His knuckles have turned white. He shouts above the roar of the storm to Mrs. Noah, "Honey, please pray for me that I'll hold out faithful to the end." Poor old Noah never would have made it.

Thank God it wasn't that way at all. God said to Noah, "Come thou and all thy house into the ark" (Gen. 7:1). These words, "come into" mean that God was already inside that ark inviting Noah to come in with Him. It was then that God shut the door and sealed it shut. Not only did He shut the water out, but at the same time He closed Noah in with Himself. Noah was as safe as the ark itself was safe, because he was in the ark. We are likewise in Christ. We'll go down if He goes down.

It seems to be that all Christians believe in some kind of security. Most of them believe their security will begin when they get to heaven. They picture themselves stepping over the threshold of the celestial city, heaving a sigh of relief and saying, "I made it! I'm safe!"

But wait a moment! No one is safe just because he is in heaven. The Scripture teaches that the glorious angels fell from heaven. Don't you see that security is not in a place but in a Person? His name is Jesus. He is our ark of safety. You see we have something that even angels don't have. I had rather be a saved sinner than an innocent angel. We are safe in Christ and that is the only safety we have.

## The Predestination of the Saint

And we know that all things work together for good to them that love God, to them who are the called according to his purpose. For whom he did foreknow, he also did predestinate to be conformed to the image of his Son, that he might be the first-born among many brethren. Moreover whom he did predestinate, them he also called: and whom he called, them he also justified: and whom he justified, them he also glorified (Rom. 8:28–30).

The child of God, according to this Scripture, has been foreknown in the mind of God before the foundation of the world. Now the theologians have debated and dialogued in the discussion of predestination for ages. And there have been some farfetched interpretations. Some feel that every event of our lives has been minutely programmed ahead of time, and there is nothing that we can do to change it. The story is told of a little old lady who fell down the cellar stairs, got up, brushed herself off, and said, "I'm glad that's over with." I don't believe in that kind of predestination, but I do believe that God will carry out His great, eternal purposes in the lives of every man and woman, boy and girl who places faith in Jesus Christ.

I'm writing these words on a 727 jet above St. Louis while I'm headed for Oklahoma City. My actions on this airplane are more or less of my own choosing, but yet the plane is headed to a predetermined destination. It is, humanly speaking, predestined for Oklahoma City.

Now, the airlines can't always make it to their predetermined destinations; but what God predestines, He fulfills. I am predestined to be "conformed to the image of his Son" and all hell cannot stop it. As a matter of fact, the Scripture speaks of me as having already been glorified. Actually, the verb is in the past tense. It says that whom He called, "them he also justified, and whom he justified, them he also glorified." I don't have to wait until I die to see whether or not I am going to heaven.

In the council halls of eternity, I have already been glorified. In the heart and mind of God it is already done. What has been settled in eternity cannot be undone in time. What has been decreed by heaven cannot be annulled by hell. Anyone predestined to be conformed to the image of God's Son is as secure as he could possibly be.

## The Present Tense of Salvation

Eternal life means life that will never end. The believer has eternal life; he has life that is endless.

Consider this carefully. Eternal life does not begin for the Christian when he dies. It begins when he believes. "Verily, verily, I say unto you, He that heareth my word, and believeth on him that sent me, hath everlasting life, and shall not come into condemnation, but is passed from death unto life" (John 5:24). This verse clearly tells me that I now have eternal life. If I now have eternal life, how could I ever cease to exist with God? How could I ever again be a lost soul?

If a man were a Christian for ten years and then became a lost soul, all he would have had was "ten-year life." Whatever you have, if you ever lose it, it is not eternal. Thank God that the believer is passed from death unto life and the life he now has is eternal and everlasting.

## The Prayers of the Savior

Another reason for our security in the Lord Jesus is the intercession of our dear Savior. The finished work of Jesus was His atonement on the cross. As He was dying in agony and blood, these words burst from His bruised lips, "It is finished" (John 19:30). And thank God it was! That was the perfect sacrifice of which we have already spoken.

But not only is there the finished work of the Savior, there is also His unfinished work. "Wherefore he is able also to save them to the uttermost that come unto God by him, seeing he ever liveth to make intercession for them" (Heb. 7:25).

Christ is ever living and ever interceding. And how He intercedes and prays for His own is seen in His great, high-priestly prayer in John 17. Notice the ones for whom Jesus is interceding. "I pray for them: I pray not for the world, but for them whom thou hast given me, for they are thine" (John 17:9). It is clear that He is praying for His own, the saints, His born-again ones.

And what is He praying for them? "I pray not that thou shouldest take them out of the world, but that thou shouldest keep them from the evil" (John 17:15). He is praying for their keeping, for their eternal security. And we know that when He prayed for their security, He was heard; for He himself said, "thou hearest me always" (John 11:42). He never prayed a prayer that was not answered. So that clearly means that those whom He has prayed for will be securely kept.

Here is the exciting part for us. He was not just praying for those early disciples—Peter, James, and John and His other contemporaries. He, by faith, looked down through the tunnel of time and prayed for you and for me. Listen to this. "Neither pray I for these alone, but for them also which shall believe on me through their word" (John 17:20). He might as well have inserted our names.

The intercessory work of Jesus is illustrated by an episode in the life of Simon Peter. Peter was weak in the flesh, but he had a heart full of faith in Christ. Jesus, knowing his weakness, predicted that he would three times deny his Lord. But here is the comforting part. Jesus said, "But I have prayed for thee, that thy faith fail not" (Luke 22:32). Though Peter stumbled, he did not utterly fall. He was weak, but Jesus had prayed for him; and his faith did not fall. The cowardly Peter went on to become the apostle of Pentecost.

I might note right here that Jesus never prayed such prayers for Judas. Peter had placed his faith in Christ, but Judas had never done so. "But there are some of you that believe not. For Jesus knew from the beginning who they were that believed not, and who should betray him" (John 6:64). "He spoke of Judas Iscariot the son of Simon: for he it was that should betray him, being one of the twelve" (John 6:71).

Judas never lost his salvation for he had no salvation to lose. He never was a believer. There was a fundamental difference between Judas and Peter. Judas may have looked better outwardly, but Peter had a heart of faith. And because he did, Jesus interceded for him. People like us, weak as we are, have a Savior who ever lives to make intercession. What a security we have.

I know that I am weak but, thank God, in spite of my weakness and sin, there is none who can condemn me. "Who is he that condemneth? . . . It is Christ that died, yea rather, that is risen again, who is even at the right hand of God, who also maketh intercession for us" (Rom. 8:34). In the face of the accuser is the perfect answer—the upraised and pierced hand of my Intercessor.

## The Power of God's Sovereignty

Blessed be the God and Father of our Lord Jesus Christ, which according to his abundant mercy hath begotten us again unto a lively hope by the resurrection of Jesus Christ from the dead. To an inheritance incorruptible, and undefiled, and that fadeth not away, reserved in heaven for you, Who are kept by the power of God through faith unto salvation ready to be revealed in the last time" (1 Pet. 1:3–5).

We are kept by the power of God! What a comforting thought. Is there a loving parent anywhere who would not preserve his children from death or disaster if it were in his power to do so? Yet as parents we fail often because we do not have the power to perform our heart's desire. This is never true, however, with almighty God. He has the power to keep His children.

In Romans 8 we have already seen that we are predestined for glory. But Romans 8 goes on to teach that because we are *predestined* for glory, we are *preserved* for glory.

### No Fault Can Defile Us

Who shall lay any thing to the charge of God's elect? . . . It is God that justifieth. Who is he that condemneth? . . . It is Christ that died, yea rather, that is risen again, who is even at the right hand of God, who also maketh intercession for us (Rom. 8:33,34).

### No Foe Can Destroy Us

Who shall separate us from the love of Christ? . . . shall tribulation, or distress, or persecution, or famine, or nakedness, or peril, or sword? . . . As it is written, For thy sake we are killed all the day long; we are accounted as sheep for the slaughter. Nay, in all these things we are more than conquerors through him that loved us (Rom. 8:35–37).

### No Fear Need Discourage Us

For I am persuaded, that neither death, nor life, nor angels, nor principalities, nor powers, nor things present, nor things to come, Nor height, nor depth, nor any other creature, shall be able to separate us from the love of God, which is in Christ Jesus our Lord (Rom. 8:38,39).

All of the enemies of the Christian do not separate him from the Lord, but only draw him all the closer. This marvelous eighth chapter of Romans begins with *no con-*

*demnation* and ends with *no separation.* Oh, that people would understand what a wonderful salvation they have in the Lord Jesus Christ. He moves into our hearts to stay.

Some may call this teaching of the security of the believer a dangerous doctrine. But, friend, if it is true, it cannot possibly be dangerous. The reasoning of those who feel that there is a danger in teaching security is this: They feel that the Christian, feeling that he is secure, will relax and let his guard down and enter into a sinful lifestyle. Sometimes it is put like this: "If I believed in eternal security, then I would get saved and sin all I want to."

There are two fatal flaws in this line of reasoning. One is that when a person says that he wants to sin, he is giving evidence that he has never been saved at all. May I say that I sin all I want to. As a matter of fact, I sin more than I want to, because *I don't want to.* God knows how often I fail, but from the time I said an everlasting yes to Jesus to this moment there has been in my heart a desire to live a holy life. If you still want to sin, you need a new birth. With the new birth, you will get a "new want."

Also, we need not think that security is a license to sin with impunity. The heavenly Father will surely chastise His children if they are disobedient. "For whom the Lord loveth he chasteneth, and scourgeth every son whom he receiveth. If ye endure chastening, God dealeth with you as with sons; for what son is he whom the father chasteneth not?" (Heb. 12:6,7).

That chastisement may take many forms. It may be the sense of broken fellowship. It may be the loss of joy. It may mean that our prayers do not get through. It may mean a loss of health or prosperity.

But even in all of this the Father is dealing in love. It is comforting to know He loves us enough to chastise us. And it is also so very comforting to know that He has promised, "I will never leave thee nor forsake thee" (Heb. 13:5).

# The Golden Key
# of Faith

*Paul's prayer for the Ephesians was "That Christ may dwell in your hearts by faith" (Eph. 3:17). The door through which Jesus enters the human heart—and thereby makes you His temple— swings upon the hinges of grace, and faith is the key that unlocks that door.*

In this final chapter we will think together about faith. This golden key of faith opens not only the door of the heart to Jesus but also the door of heaven's riches to the believer.

All of God's blessings come to us through faith. Jesus said, "According to your faith be it unto you" (Matt. 9:29). Therefore, the bench mark of blessing is not according to our feelings, friends, fame, or fortune but according to our faith. The measure of accomplishment in the Christian life is always faith.

Conversely, most of the problems of the Christian's life are caused by lack of faith. *Worry*, for instance, is the opposite of faith. Worry is an insult to God. Worrying is like saying, "God, I don't think You can handle this one." *Loneliness* is the result of not believing in God's presence. Faith makes God's presence very real to us when no one else is near. Unbelief, however, leaves us isolated even in a crowd. Many people are haunted by the ghost of *guilt* because of a lack of confidence in the full forgiveness of God's grace.

Faith is our acceptance of God's acceptance of us. *Disobedience* results from lack of faith in what God has said. It is human nature to touch the wet paint when the sign says, "Wet Paint." We are not quite sure that it is wet, so we check for ourselves. If we truly believe God's "wet paint" signs in His Word, however, we will not so easily transgress.

## The Description of Faith

The Book of Hebrews contains a mighty message on this vital subject of faith.

> Now faith is the substance of things hoped for, the evidence of things not seen. For by it the elders obtained a good report (Heb. 11:1,2).

To my knowledge, there is no definition of faith given in the Scriptures. The verses above are a description rather than a definition of faith, but they make clear what faith is in the life of the believer.

Faith is not positive thinking. It is not following a hunch. It is not a feeling of optimism. It is not hoping for the best. All of these may be well and good in their place, but they are not biblical faith.

### Faith Is Substance

"Now faith is the substance of things hoped for" (Heb. 11:1).

Substance means "solid ground." The English word gives the meaning of the Greek quite well. "Sub-stans" means there is something beneath us to stand upon. When we are living by faith, we are not walking on eggshells and Jello. We are standing upon Solid Rock.

Sometimes the modern materialist will say, "Don't talk to

me about faith. Talk about real things." By "real" he means the things that can be experienced with the five senses—the things we can see, smell, hear, taste, or feel.

But are these things all that are real? Paul reminds us ". . . the things which are seen are temporal; but the things which are not seen are eternal" (2 Cor. 4:18). Which is the more real—that which is temporary or that which is eternal?

### Faith Is Evidence

"Now faith is . . . the evidence of things not seen" (Heb. 11:1). This means that faith is the *convincing proof* that God will keep His Word.

Evidence is the proof of unseen reality. There can be no evidence without the reality that has caused the evidence. It is so important that we understand this. If we do, we shall see the difference between real and synthetic faith.

There is a counterfeit faith in the land today that is really nothing more than positive thinking couched in religious terms. Here is how the prophets of synthetic faith explain faith. They say, "God is able to do anything. Therefore, if you have enough faith, He will do anything for you. All you have to do is *name it and claim it.*"

That sounds good, but it bears little resemblance to biblical faith. We do not "name it and claim it." We cannot legitimately claim it until God has named it. What I mean by that is, faith is our response to a revelation of God's will by His Word and His Spirit. "So then faith cometh by hearing, and hearing by the word of God" (Rom. 10:17).

Believing does not make it so. Faith does not bring anything into existence. Faith is the evidence of things that are already in the heart and mind of God. I cannot truly believe until a thing is settled. Anything else is but positive thinking or wishful desire. Faith is the evidence in my heart that God has spoken.

## The Dynamics of Faith

But without faith it is impossible to please him: for he that cometh to God must believe that he is, and that he is a rewarder of them that diligently seek him (Heb. 11:6).

Faith is the most dynamic force in the world because it releases the hand of omnipotency. The above verse gives us insight into the mighty power of faith. There are two major thoughts in this verse.

### By Faith Man Gives God Pleasure

"Without faith it is impossible to please Him . . ." (Heb. 11:6). There should be no greater aim in life than to please God. For if we please God, it really doesn't matter whom we displease and if we displease God, it really doesn't matter whom we please. There is no pleasing God without believing God.

Why is this so? Why is God so pleased with faith? Why didn't He just create man so that man would automatically believe in Him? Why doesn't He do something to prove Himself to us?

Have no doubts about it. If God wanted to prove Himself, He would have no difficulty doing so. He could roll back the heavens and make Himself known with a display of His grandeur, might, and glory. There would not be one unbeliever left upon the earth. However, faith would not be necessary then.

One day, God will reveal Himself in just that way. But it will not be to save men but rather to judge them. At that time, every knee shall bow and every tongue shall confess, but it will be a fearful and awful day. In this day and age,

God refuses to reveal Himself in that manner because He wants us to respond to Him by faith.

The reason God demands faith is that faith is a moral response to the character of God. Faith gives God the honor that is due His Name.

Let me illustrate this. A rich person may have many so-called friends, but in the back of his mind he may be wondering, "Do these people love me for who I am or for what I have?" No one wants to be used without being loved.

Likewise, God wants us to love Him, not for what He has or for what He can do, but for who He is. Therefore, God refuses to bribe us or overwhelm us in order that we might follow Him.

This helps us understand why Jesus came into the world as He did. He came to reveal the character of God, not to display the grandeur of God. He left all of the splendor and glory and majesty that was inherently His in heaven when He came to this earth. Isaiah said of Him, ". . . he hath no form nor comeliness; and when we shall see him, there is no beauty that we should desire him" (Is. 53:2).

This means that Jesus did not ride out of heaven in a jeweled chariot, wearing regal robes and a diadem on His brow. Rather, He was born in a smelly stable with cow dung on the floor. He was reared in an obscure village as a carpenter's son. He lived a life of poverty and humility.

It is true that He performed miracles but not in order to get followers. His miracles were works of mercy and revelations of truth, but they were not cheap tricks nor public-relations stunts. They were not done to get a following. Often He would say after a miracle, "Don't tell anyone about this."

Jesus knew the mind-set of the miraclemongers—those who wanted Him to give them a sign from heaven so they could believe. These were the ones who followed Him for a while after He had fed the five thousand. But when He preached to them about real commitment, they left Him.

Yet, there were others who loved and followed Jesus sincerely. They did not follow Him primarily for what He did or for what He had, but rather for who He was. They responded by faith to His character and person.

There is something about a right heart that responds to God by faith like the eye responds to light when it functions correctly and like the ear responds to sound when the ear is healthy.

The reason, therefore, that God honors faith is that faith honors God. Faith is a moral response to the character of God. It, therefore, above all things gives God pleasure.

Look at it from the other side. A lack of faith or unbelief greatly displeases God. Unbelief is a vile and wicked sin. Really there is no greater sin. It is the parent sin. It is the sin out of which all other sins grow.

Unbelief is really the one sin that keeps a person out of heaven. Jesus said, "For God sent not his Son into the world to condemn the world; but that the world through him might be saved. He that believeth on him is not condemned: but he that believeth not is condemned already, because he hath not believed in the name of the only begotten Son of God" (John 3:17,18).

This sin of unbelief is so terrible because of what it says about the character of God. Suppose you are introduced to a group as a speaker. The Master of Ceremonies says many nice things about you but then adds, "There is one thing I must tell you about our speaker. You cannot believe what he says." It would not matter then how many nice things he had said. When he said you were not believable, he cut the taproot of your character.

It matters not how many nice things you may say about God if you do not believe Him. What difference does it make how we speak of the greatness of God or of His love when we refuse to believe He is worthy of our faith. ". . . he that believeth not God has made him a liar . . ." (1 John 5:10).

Someone may protest and say that he cannot believe because he has genuine, intellectual problems. "It is not my fault if I cannot believe," he says. But it is his fault. Unbelief is a moral sin not an intellectual problem. It starts in the heart not in the head. It may show up in the head, but that is only a symptom of what is in the heart. "Take heed, brethren, lest there be in any of you an evil heart of unbelief, in departing from the living God" (Heb. 3:12).

A man came to see me concerning his wife. She was suicidal, and he wanted me to counsel with her. I said I would if he would come with her to my study. This man worked in the space industry at Cape Kennedy and held an important position.

The wife poured out her story of a broken heart. She wept as she spoke of her husband's cruelty, infidelity, drunkenness, and gambling. I turned to him and asked, "Sir, are you a Christian?" Mind you, I was not asking for information but turning the conversation toward Christ.

He threw back his head and laughed scornfully. "No, I am an atheist," he said.

"Well," I responded, "an atheist is one who knows there is no God. Do you know all there is to know?"

"Of course not," he shot back.

"Would it be generous to say you know half of all there is to know?"

"Yes, that would be very generous," he muttered.

"Then if you only know half of all there is to know, wouldn't you have to admit the possibility that God may exist in the body of knowledge you do not have?" I asked.

"I never thought of that," he said. "Well, I am not an atheist, then. I am an agnostic."

I said, "Now we are getting somewhere. Agnosticism means you don't know." (I didn't tell him that the Latin equivalent for agnostic is ignoramus.) "An agnostic is a doubter," I said.

"Well, that is what I am and a big one."

"I don't care what size as much as what kind. There are two kinds of doubters you know—honest and dishonest. The honest doubter doesn't know, but he wants to know. The dishonest doubter doesn't know because he doesn't want to know. He can't find God for the very same reason that a thief can't find a policeman. Which kind of doubter are you?" I asked.

His face softened. "I never really thought about it. I guess I never really wanted to know," he said.

"Did you know that there is a promise to the honest doubter in God's Word?" I asked. I then read to him the words of Jesus who was speaking to the doubters of His day. "Jesus answered them, and said, My doctrine is not mine, but his that sent me. If any man will do his will, he shall know of the doctrine, whether it be of God, or whether I speak of myself" (John 7:16,17).

I continued, "In plain English that says that if a man will surrender his will completely, God will reveal Himself to that man." My friend was getting interested.

I then asked him, "Would you be willing to sign a statement like this: God, I don't know whether You exist or not, but I want to know and because I want to know I will make an honest investigation and because it is an honest investigation, I will follow the results of that investigation wherever they lead me regardless of the cost."

After a time of soul searching, he said, "Yes, I would be willing to sign a statement like that. I will do it. How do I go about making such an investigation?"

We shared together, and I got him started reading the Gospel of John with the commitment that he really wanted to know the truth and would follow any truth revealed to him regardless of the personal cost or consequences.

In a matter of weeks this same man came back to my study, got on his knees, and gave his heart to Christ. That was many years ago. I had lost track of him until recently, when I received a letter from him. He is now living in a northern state and is an excited witness for Christ.

In his letter to me, he said, "Dear Friend, thank you for being willing to spend time with this general in the devil's army."

Now where was this man's real problem? It was not in his head as he first thought, but in his heart. When he surrendered his will, faith followed. Unbelief reveals a wicked heart.

### Through Faith, God Gives Man Treasure

Hebrews 11:6 tells us that when we believe God "he is a rewarder of them that diligently seek him." Our God longs to show Himself mighty on behalf of people who trust Him. Faith is the key to meeting our needs, whatever those needs may be. Let me list a few of the needs that faith can supply.

*Salvation.* "Therefore being justified by faith, we have peace with God through our Lord Jesus Christ" (Rom. 5:1).

*The fullness of the Spirit.* "That the blessing of Abraham might come to the Gentiles through Jesus Christ; that we might receive the promise of the Spirit through faith" (Gal. 3:14).

*Victory over the world.* ". . . and this is the victory that overcometh the world, even our faith" (1 John 5:4).

*Victory over Satan.* "Above all, taking the shield of faith, wherewith ye shall be able to quench all of the fiery darts of the wicked" (Eph. 6:16).

*Answered prayer.* "Therefore I say unto you, What things soever ye desire, when ye pray, believe that ye receive them, and ye shall have them" (Mark 11:24).

There is an imagined story of a scene in heaven. Some angels approach the throne and say, "Father, there is a mortal on earth asking for a blessing. What is your pleasure concerning his request?" The Father asked, "What did he send his faith in?" The angels answered, "He sent his faith in a thimble." The Father says, "Well, fill the thimble with blessings and send it back to him. According to his faith, be it unto him."

Again, the angels come and say, "Father, another mortal is asking blessings of Thee." The Father asked, "And what did he send his faith in?" The angels respond, "He sent his faith in a huge barrel." With a smile the Father says, "Fill the barrel with blessings and send it back to him. According to his faith, be it unto him."

By faith man gives God pleasure, and through faith God gives man treasure.

## The Development of Faith

Wherefore seeing we also are compassed about with so great a cloud of witnesses, let us lay aside every weight, and the sin which doth so easily beset us, and let us run with patience the race that is set before us, Looking unto Jesus the author and finisher of our faith; who for the joy that was set before him endured the cross, despising the shame, and is set down at the right hand of the throne of God (Heb. 12:1,2).

These verses tell us how to develop our faith. The writer of Hebrews has given an entire chapter on what others have done by faith, and then he speaks to us. The idea is that now they (the heroes of the faith) are in the heavenly grandstand and we as spiritual athletes are in the arena to run the race of faith.

There are some simple rules given in Hebrews 12:1,2 that tell us how to develop a dynamic faith.

1. *Saturate your heart and mind with the Word of God.* Notice the word "wherefore" in Hebrews 12:1. It refers us to what has already been said.

The entire eleventh chapter of Hebrews is devoted to the subject of faith, and it contains references to almost all of the Old Testament. The point is that the Bible is a book for developing your faith. Remember Romans 10:17, "So then faith cometh by hearing, and hearing by the word of God."

The Bible may need explaining, but it is not first and foremost a book to be explained but a book to be believed.

The Bible may be admired, but the promises of the Bible are not so much mottoes to be hung on the wall as they are checks to be carried to the bank of heaven and cashed.

Would you have faith? Love the Bible, study it, memorize it, meditate on it, obey it, and you will find faith welling up in your heart.

2. *Repent of all known sin.* Hebrews 12:1 says, ". . . let us lay aside every weight and the sin which doth so easily beset us. . . ." An athlete is foolish who endeavors to run with excess baggage or anything that would cause him to stumble. The words, "easily beset" have the meaning in the original language of cleverly placing something around an object. Sin can cleverly place itself around us so as to cause us to stumble in the race of faith.

Remember that unbelief comes from an evil heart. If you are having difficulty believing God, it may be that unconfessed sin is tripping you up.

In the Bible, God mentions grace and peace several times together, but always grace comes before peace for that is God's order. We cannot know peace until we have experienced grace.

Likewise, God mentions repentance and faith in that same sequence. If you are having difficulty with faith, you should try repentance. It always comes first. Remember that faith and sin are mutually exclusive.

3. *Use the faith that you already have.* We are told to "run with patience the race that is set before us" (Heb. 12:1). I like the word "run" because it indicates what faith is. Faith is active not static. It is more than mere belief. Faith is belief with legs on it.

The athlete learns to run by running. Books about running are not enough. Lectures on running will not suffice. He must get out on the track and begin to learn. Use the weak faith that you have, and it will become stronger faith.

To change the figure of speech for a moment, let me remind you that Jesus said faith is like a mustard seed. What is so great about a mustard seed is that though it may be tiny, it has God-given life in it. It is meant not to be treasured but to be planted so that it will produce so much more. It has been well said that any fool can count the seeds in an apple but only God can count the apples in a seed.

Take the faith that you have now and get it into action. It will grow as you exercise it. It will produce as you plant it.

4. *Keep your eyes on Jesus.* We are told to be "Looking unto Jesus the author and finisher of our faith . . ." (Heb. 12:2). Faith is the by-product of keeping one's eyes upon Jesus.

The word "looking" is *aphorao* in the Greek language and it means "looking away from all else unto a certain object." Take your eyes from self, Satan, and circumstances and turn them to Jesus.

The word also speaks of dependence and trust. We are to look *unto* Jesus. Suppose you had a financial need and your friend said, "Look to me. I will take care of it." He would not mean that you were to look at him but that you were to depend upon him.

Dear friend, Jesus is indeed so very wonderful. He alone is the Author and Finisher of our faith. Let His glory and beauty fill your heart right now. Look to Him for every need.

# Notes

Chapter 1
[1]Ian Thomas, *The Saving Life of Christ* (Grand Rapids, Mich.: Zondervan, 1961), p. 19.

Chapter 7
[1]*Moody Monthly* (April, 1975), p. 61.

Chapter 9
[1]Earl D. Radmacher, *You and Your Thoughts* (Wheaton, Ill.: Tyndale, 1977).
[2]Jack Van Impe and Roger F. Campbell, *Alcohol: the Beloved Enemy* (Nashville: Thomas Nelson, 1980).
[3]Ibid.

Chapter 10
[1]Angel Martinez, *The Fountain of Youth* (Grand Rapids: Zondervan, 1957, o.p.), p. 104.